ANXIETY:

DEBUG IT

DON'T DRUG IT!

by

Dr. Michael Catchpole

Anxiety: Debug It Don't Drug It

Copyright © Michael Catchpole 2019
Author: Dr. Michael Catchpole
Publisher: Rutherford Press

For information, contact:
          Rutherford Press,
          PO Box 648
          Qualicum Beach, BC, Canada V9K 1A0
          info@rutherfordpress.ca
          https://rutherfordpress.ca

  ISBN (book)   # 978-1-988739-36-6
  ISBN (ebook)   # 978-1-988739-37-3

CONTENTS

Anxiety

Anxiety

About The Author

Dr. Michael Catchpole has been involved in the international distribution of evidence-based psychological knowledge for 40 years and continues to be unwaveringly active in this process. His particular expertise is in the areas of anxiety and the anxiety-related disorders.

Dr. Catchpole worked in private practice as a Registered Psychologist for 25 years seeing adults with a variety of psychological disorders. Amongst his clients were the Royal Canadian Mounted Police, WorkSafe British Columbia, the Canadian Armed Forces, the Nuu-Chah-Nulth Tribal Council and various other private and public sector organizations and individuals.

Dr. Catchpole earned a PhD in Psychology from the University of British Columbia in 1977 and has been a full time psychology professor at North Island College for 41 years. Additionally, for the last 23 years, he has taught Disability Management courses for Pacific Coast University for Workplace Health Sciences focusing particularly on effective return to work strategies for those who have developed psychological disabilities. He has delivered over 200 workshops on psychology-related topics for various school, parent, rehabilitation and police groups.

In 1988 the British Columbia Psychological Association awarded Dr. Catchpole the Donald Sampson Master Teacher award for his pioneering work in educational television and public education in the field of psychology. In 2004 he won the Adjudicators' Award from the British Columbia Innovations in Educational Technology Group for long term career achievement in the application of technology in educational delivery. In February of 2011 Dr. Catchpole was awarded the Parke O. Davidson Award from the BC Psychological Association for Significant and Substantive Contributions to the Practice and Profession of Psychology. In 2014 the Washington DC-based Instructional Technology Council, an affiliated council of the American Association of Community Colleges, awarded Dr. Catchpole its Lifetime Achievement Award. This award is given each year at the ITC's E-Learning conference to an exemplary leader who has made a lifetime contribution to innovation within the field of distance learning and knowledge distribution.

Through his production company, Harrison, Catchpole and Associates, Dr. Catchpole has engaged in numerous video and DVD projects. He added 13 video interviews with experts on adult and child anxiety to the website of the non-profit organization, AnxietyBC (now AnxietyCanada). He also has produced and hosted three, one-hour educational DVDs on self-treatment of psychological disorders. These DVDs include:

Separation Anxiety: A Parents' Guide;

Obsessive-Compulsive Disorder: A Parent's Guide; and

Effectively Managing Panic Disorder.

Anxiety

Acknowledgement

I would like to thank the many psychologists, medical professionals, friends and former students who reviewed this manuscript and provided invaluable comments and edits. In particular I would like to thank my close friend Mr. Robert Starke for his very helpful micro and macro edit suggestions during the preparation of this manuscript. Additionally I would like to thank my former and very talented student, Shane Meyer for his help with the literature review. I would also like to thank Samantha Barrowcliff, Linda Sneed and Heather Thompson for their helpful comments on earlier drafts of the manuscript.

Additionally, I would like to express my thanks to North Island College for their unwavering support of my efforts to distribute evidence-based, psychological knowledge to students and the public no matter how remote or challenging their circumstances.

I also wish to say a very special thank you to Dr. Maureen Whittal who provided a detailed scientific review of the manuscript as well as offering numerous invaluable suggestions.

Finally I want to thank my three daughters for their exceptionally useful advice throughout this process as well as my psychologist wife, Dr. Linda Harrison for her support during the preparation of this manuscript. For the last 45 years she has been much of the secret "steak" behind whatever "sizzle" I may possess.

Michael Catchpole, PhD

March 2019

Forward

It is such a pleasure to be asked to contribute to this book. It is the culmination of decades of Dr. Catchpole's experience in treating people with anxiety disorders and teaching students the finer points of psychology. Anxiety disorders are among the most common mental health conditions. One in four people in their lifetime will struggle with levels of anxiety that interfere with how they live their lives. Cognitive behavior therapy (CBT) is an effective psychological approach to help people improve the quality of their lives and decrease the impact of anxiety. CBT is a widely studied form of therapy with thousands of people participating in research trials worldwide. Everything that you will read in this book was tested and proven effective.

One of the biggest things in managing anxiety is the trade off between short term gain and long term consequences. Anxiety sufferers and the people who love them (and sadly some "helping" professions) often opt for short term solutions that ease anxiety. Unfortunately, these quick fixes result in anxiety that is worse in the long run. Learning to manage anxiety is to reverse this trade off. Doing what is difficult and scary in the short term will make anxiety better in the long term. This book will lay out how to take these steps.

As Dr. Catchpole points out, there is an art to doing CBT. Having effective tools is not sufficient; the therapist delivering the tools needs to do it in a way that inspires trust and confidence. I know for my own career, the confidence with which I delivered treatment grew over the years as I witnessed people improving and learning to manage their anxiety. CBT works! Dr. Catchpole likewise writes with a great deal of confidence. He believes in CBT because he has decades of seeing people improve using the strategies he has so concisely discussed in the pages that follow.

As you read this book, please know that you are following the advice of a hugely well-respected psychologist and master clinician who has helped hundreds and hundreds of people live better, more fulfilling lives with less anxiety. I wish you well in your journey!

Maureen L Whittal, PhD., ABPP
Co-founder Anxiety Canada
Co-Chair Anxiety Canada Scientific Advisory Committee

Clinical Associate Professor (Psychiatry), University of British Columbia

Anxiety

PREFACE

Why I Wrote This Book

Since earning a PhD in psychology in 1977 I have had three career goals.

The first has been to use the best of evidence-based, psychotherapeutic techniques to help my clients master their anxiety and anxiety-related disorders. Please note my use of the word "client" rather than "patient". The word "patient" is from the Latin, "patiens", meaning passive. The last thing you want to be when working to bring about positive change in your life is passive, hence "client" is a much better description of the relationship one has with one's psychologist. This reminds me of the old joke. "How many psychologists does it take to change a lightbulb?" The answer is "Only one, but the lightbulb has to want to change." Since you have been brave enough to buy and begin reading this book I hope and predict that, together we can brighten your particular world.

My second career objective has been to make every effort to distribute, as widely as possible, the very best of scientifically valid, psychological knowledge to clients, students and the general public. Whenever possible, I have brought the top researchers and practitioners in the field into my presentations and I would like to publicly thank all these professionals for their generous donations of time and expertise. Over the course of my career I have been lucky enough to be given access to a wide range of opportunities to distribute psychological knowledge. Amongst these have been face-to-face teaching, seminars, workshops, on-line instruction, broadcast television, video-conferencing and most recently DVD's and video streaming. This book seemed the next logical step.

Psychology is a rigorous scientific discipline but, as is also problematic for medicine, there are a great many quacks, charlatans and "snake oil" salespeople on its periphery. This book will focus on actual, scientifically validated treatments, and aims to save you from wasting your time and money on "psychoquackery" of which, unfortunately, there is so much.

My third and final career goal has been to convince the public, and more directly in this book, *to prove to you* that it is no longer necessary for you to live with or be bullied by distressing levels of anxiety.

This book will focus on nine anxiety-related disorders, which include: Panic Disorder, Agoraphobia, Social Anxiety Disorder, a Specific Phobia, Hoarding Disorder, Body-Focused Repetitive Disorder, Generalized Anxiety Disorder, Obsessive-Compulsive and Post-Traumatic Stress Disorder. All these types of anxiety can be mastered and I will show you how in the following chapters.

You will recall the slogan "Cancer can be beaten". To this I will add, "Anxiety-related Disorders **have** been beaten". All these disorders are now proven to be treatable, and the success rates, if you follow the Cognitive Behavioral Therapy (CBT) model I will outline in this book, are outstanding.

If you are able to add a CBT trained psychologist to your team, progress will be easier. You may wish to double check their qualifications as many therapists say they do CBT but few actually know how to do it properly. Credentialing sources you could ask about might include the Academy of Cognitive Therapy or, if you are in Canada, the Canadian Association of Cognitive Behavioral Therapy. Having said that, if you can't involve a professional in your treatment then, regardless, there is ample guidance in this book for you to bring about a substantial reduction, if not complete removal of your distress.

There are also several excellent self-treatment CBT workbooks on the market that will assist you. I will refer you to these resources in Part II of this book. One resource I would like to mention now, as you may wish to consult it as you read this book, is the website www.anxietycanada.com. I was fortunate enough to be asked to make some contributions to the development of this site.

Finally, I want to stress that this book is not only intended to help you to manage your anxiety and anxiety-related disorders but also to set you free to really enjoy your life to the fullest. As I'll explain in Chapter 3, once anxiety no longer controls your life or limits your freedom, you will come to understand that it can be viewed as a useful tool, one that signals an opportunity to grow, rather than something to avoid. Anxiety, well managed, truly is the edge of personal growth and a life without growth is not much of a life at all.

Disclaimer

I have made every effort to support the content of this manuscript with evidence-based, fully replicated research studies. These studies may be found in the Works Cited section. I also want to be clear that the opinions expressed in this book are mine alone own and do not necessarily reflect those of my family, friends or professional colleagues. In addition, any case studies that I have included in this book are heavily-disguised composites of the many clients I have seen over the years and do not describe any particular individual. Professionals in the field will note that I have not included two recent additions to the adult anxiety-related disorders (Separation Anxiety Disorder and Illness Anxiety Disorder) but encourage you to read up on them.

I also want to stress that if your anxiety is paired with high levels of depression and suicidal ideation it is important that you involve a family physician in your treatment.

PART I

WHAT ANXIETY REALLY IS

AND HOW TO MASTER IT

A Quick Note To The Reader

In writing this book I am attempting to reach two audiences:

One is that group of MDs, PhDs and other mental health professionals involved directly or indirectly in helping people who struggle with the anxiety-related disorders. For this group of readers I have laid out what I believe to be a convincing, evidence-based argument that in cases of mild and moderate anxiety, "debugging" the mind is a far more effective and long-lasting way

Anxiety

to help anxiety sufferers than drugging their brains. For more severe forms of anxiety the literature indicates that adding anti-depressant medication to CBT may add to treatment success.

Chapters 1, 2 and 5, in particular, are designed to make that "de-bugging not drugging" case. Chapters 3, 4 and 6, as well as Part II, should also be of value to these readers when it comes to setting effective treatment plans.

The second group of readers I have written this book for are those of you that are, **right now,** living a less-than-full life because you are currently being imprisoned by the **bully** known as anxiety. Since you readers may well wish to "get on with it" and begin knocking down the walls of your imprisonment I am going to suggest that, if you wish, you could consider beginning with Chapters 3, 4 and 6 as well as the relevant chapters in Part II of this book. You readers also, of course, are very welcome to read Chapters 1, 2 and 5 and I hope you will do so, especially if you have already tried medication and found it wanting.

Happy reading to all and thank you for selecting this book.

CHAPTER 1

YOUR MIND CANNOT BE ILL

In this first chapter I am going to make the case that if you currently suffer from anxiety, or an anxiety-related disorder, you are *not* "mentally ill".

I will go on to explain that, in fact, it is impossible for your mind to be ill at all. Yes, your *brain* can be diseased or dysfunctional, as is the case for schizophrenia, dementia or bipolar disorder, for example, but not your *mind*. I realize this is a provocative statement but allow me to elaborate.

Anxiety

I will begin by drawing a key and very important distinction between a disrupted mind and an ill brain. Let's embark upon this process by looking back over time and examine how societies have viewed those people who thought or acted in "abnormal" ways.

A Short History of "Abnormality"

As many readers will know, for centuries when people acted strangely they were assumed to be possessed by evil spirits, the Devil and so on. Treatment of such people (if they weren't killed as a precautionary measure) therefore focused on either releasing these evil forces via trephining (drilling holes in the skull) or by torturing the body so that the spirits would leave. Hence the expression "Beat the Devil out of him". Thankfully, this approach mostly has been abandoned, though some religions continue to offer "exorcisms" and claim them to be effective. This despite numerous studies that show they are of no lasting benefit and more than occasionally fatal.

The next step in the development of how we view mental disorders happened for a remarkable reason, and that was the discovery that syphilis, if left untreated, attacks the brain and leads to insanity ("general paresis"). This discovery was the beginning of the modern mental illness/mental health model which focusses on genetic and biological causation of mental disorders.

Anxiety

Using this model, one could now view "mental" (actually, brain) disorders like schizophrenia, schizoaffective disorder, dementia and bipolar disorder as diseases or dysfunctions like those of any other body organ. Instead of being seen as "possessed", sufferers were now seen as deserving of our compassion (which they most certainly are) and best assisted medically, that is biologically. Such brain dysfunctions would therefore best be treated via the traditional medical approaches of medication, surgery and hospitalization. Treatment would be done by physicians, or psychiatrists (typically, but not always, physicians with an additional four years of training in brain dysfunctions and mental disorders).

This newer, medical model has continued to encourage major advances in treatment for the *brain-based* mental disorders. Researchers in the field (who typically hold a PhD) are engaged in ongoing work to further improve physicians' and psychiatrists' ability to treat such brain disorders medically. However, as I will explain in a moment, this bio-medical model is **not** the most effective approach for understanding or treating the nine anxiety-related disorders that are the focus of this book. While brain researchers have yet to **cure** brain diseases and dysfunctions it is certainly true that great strides have been made in the use of medications and other medical procedures to help lessen the impact of these conditions. It is important to note, however, that even for the subset of mental disorders that truly are a result of brain diseases, biological treatment alone is insufficient. Psychological and social interventions also are required.

Acknowledgement of this latter point is why the diagnostic system used in the field within North America (The Diagnostic and Statistical Manual of Mental Disorders or DSM 5), calls these brain illnesses "**mental disorders**" not "mental illnesses". Why? Because ample evidence shows that sufferers' treatment is vastly more successful if evidence-based, **psychological** interventions ("talk therapy") and **social** interventions (Interpersonal Therapy, couples or family counselling and so on) also are included in the treatment plan. Please note, by the way, that when I say "evidence-based" I mean based on the outcome of valid, scientific research, not the latest "pop" psychology fad. I will elaborate on the term "evidence-based" in Chapter 5.

A person's **brain**, then, may be dysfunctional due to disease, damage or malformation and, as a consequence, their **mind** (their

Anxiety

ability to think, feel and behave adaptively) as well as their **social relationships** also will be impacted negatively. Mental "disorder" rather than mental "illness" then, is the term professionals prefer because it points to a multi-causal (biological, psychological and social) **understanding** of mental disorders, including that *small sub-set* that are primarily brain dysfunctions. Equally important, the DSM 5 term "mental disorders" also points to a multi-modal biological, psychological and social ("biopsychosocial") approach to **treatment**.

You Are Not Your Brain: The Mind as Software

Even when it comes to that handful of mental disorders that result from brain dysfunctions the term "mental illness", while a good analogy, is still not entirely accurate. What is more accurate is that malfunctions, infections, physical damage and/or structural errors within the brain negatively impact the ability of one's mind to "run" (that is, to function) upon that diseased or dysfunctional brain "platform". Think of the brain as the physical object that is your computer or tablet. The mind is the software that runs on it and allows it to perform all the functions it does. Brain illnesses negatively affect that platform and thus compromise a mind's ability to think, to initiate behavior and to feel within a "normal" (adaptive) range.

So, yes we have a real, physical thing, our brain, that if compromised will affect our *mind's* ability to achieve our goals and to enjoy our lives. This, of course, is true of the tasks of all body organs not just the brain. Our kidneys, pancreas, liver and so on also have specific tasks that will be negatively impacted if they are diseased or damaged. The fascinating, special feature of

Anxiety

the brain, in addition to all the critical functions it performs below consciousness, is that it is the organ that allows the metaphysical *"us"* to exist. That is, it permits the existence of a **mind**… a mind that allows us to think, to feel and to behave, hopefully to our best advantage, and without hurting those around us.

And who or what is our mind? Philosophers have struggled with this question for centuries. Basically, as I have hinted at above, your mind is *you*. The deeply personal you that "runs" on the brain platform. Your mind is what allows you (the "you" reading this book, for example) to exist. It is far more than the brain protoplasm that permits that existence. I will elaborate on this below when I discuss the parallel relationship between a computer's hardware and its software, and our brain and our mind.

It is critical to note at this point in our discussion that physical problems with the brain (the psychotic or brain-based disorders, in particular) are only one small group of the nearly 300 mental disorders listed in the DSM 5 diagnostic system. Vastly more common are disorders of our mind (our "software") not those that result from problems with our brain (our "hard drive"). This much larger group, which includes the anxiety-related disorders, has little or nothing to do with brain dysfunction.

Anxiety

The Anxiety-Related Disorders

Of all the types of mental disorders listed in the DSM 5 the most common, by far, are the Anxiety-related Disorders. These "disorders", of course, are merely the more extreme end of the spectrum for each of the different types of anxiety that the anxiety-related disorders describe. Amongst them are the following: Agoraphobia, Social Anxiety Disorder, Specific Phobia Disorder, Panic Disorder, Generalized Anxiety Disorder, Hoarding Disorder and Body-Focused Repetitive Disorder), as well as Obsessive-Compulsive Disorder (OCD) and Post-Traumatic Stress Disorder (PTSD). Each of these is characterized by a distressing and maladaptive amount of **anxiety**. That is, anxiety far in excess of what the situation requires.

Let me very quickly define each for you. For the full diagnostic criteria for the anxiety-related disorders see DSM 5 (you can find it on scholargoogle.com) or go to **www.anxietycanada.com**. Let me give you a very quick definition of each:

1) *Agoraphobia* is an excessive fear of being out in public or in situations from which escape might be delayed or difficult.

2) *Social Anxiety Disorder* is extreme anxiety in certain social situations (e.g., movie theatres, being a passenger in a car).

3) *Specific Phobia Disorder* is an irrationally high anxiety response to things that are not actually dangerous (e.g., dogs, heights).

4) People suffering from *Panic Disorder* are plagued by frequent and highly distressing anxiety or "panic" attacks (the sudden onset of a variety of cardiovascular, respiratory or gastrointestinal symptoms).

5) Those with *Generalized Anxiety Disorder* suffer from constant worry about every day events in the past and future.

6) People with *Hoarding Disorder* find relief from anxiety by acquiring and saving more and more things, many of which have no practical value.

7) *Body-Focussed Repetitive Disorder* sufferers experience severe anxiety if they do not engage in self-damaging behaviors like skin picking or hair pulling.

8) Those with *Obsessive-Compulsive Disorder* may experience repetitive and unwanted thoughts, images or impulses (e.g. physically harming a loved one) and/or

Anxiety

excessive and repetitive behaviors designed to bring a sense of safety (e.g., checking or washing).

9) Finally, those with **Post Traumatic Stress Disorder** suffer from nightmares, flashbacks, and exaggerated startle response after going through a life-threatening incident.

It is these disorders, as well as anxiety in general, that are the subject of this book. In fact, I suspect virtually all of you reading this have one or more of the above nine types of anxiety, if not at a clinical level (in which you qualify for an actual DSM 5 diagnosis), then at least at a sub-clinical level. "Sub-clinical", by the way, still means that they are causing you significant distress and interfere with how you want to live your life. I will elaborate on this point in Chapter 6.

As noted above, the anxiety-related disorders are the most common of all the DSM 5 mental disorders by a considerable margin. They also represent the greatest financial cost to employers and society with countless additional people suffering in silence.

The frustrating thing is that they are also the easiest to treat successfully *if* the primary focus of that treatment is the mind and not the brain. Yet such treatment is rare. I will tell you why in a moment.

In second place, in terms of frequency, is *Major Depressive Disorder* (MDD) and its various sub-types ("features"). Substantial data shows that it too is most effectively treated over the long term via a focus on the mind rather than the brain.

My point here is that absolutely we need to continue to research and seek medications that work for the brain-based mental disorders.

However, when it comes to the anxiety-related disorders, numerous research studies clearly have demonstrated that the primary focus of treatment should be the *mind*, not the brain. And the mind, since it is not a physical entity, cannot be diseased or "ill", but it *can* be "de-bugged". We now have a large body of research showing us how to do this.

Let me explain.

Where Do Anxiety-Related Disorders Come From?

If the *brain* of someone suffering from an anxiety-related disorder is unlikely to be diseased or dysfunctional, then how do people develop such disorders? Genetic vulnerability certainly plays a role. People vary greatly in the impact environmental stressors may have upon them. Given this, how do environmental "insults" (negative events) lead to mental disorders? I think the honest answer is that we do not exactly know but we do know that a stressful experience, plus a vulnerability to that particular form of stress, is a big part of the answer. Thus, for example, seeing a child hit by a car may produce sadness in some and PTSD in others. Having an occasionally irregular heartbeat may be interpreted as no big deal by some and trigger Panic Disorder in others. In response to a marked increase in life stress some may find relief in repetitive mental rituals or checking behaviors (Obsessive-Compulsive Disorder) and others may not. Forced confinement at home subsequent to having a baby, or as a result of an injury or illness, may lead to Agoraphobia for some but not all, and so on.

What appears to happen is that certain stressful events "load" what I call "mental malware", similar to a computer "virus", into the "mental software" of our mind. In other words, such events load disruptive

> "MENTAL
>
> MALWARE"

thoughts and feelings, which then interfere with our (that is, our mind's) day-to-day functioning.

Clearly, in such cases, it is therefore the mind that needs to be treated directly and less so, *if at all*, the brain. The characteristics of these negative experiences vary greatly but each of them can lead to one of the types of anxiety that this book addresses. I will elaborate on this in Part II where I will summarize the treatment of nine of the anxiety-related disorders and refer you to some excellent resources explaining the precise, tailored treatment for each. The most effective, evidence-based model underlying these treatments, I will foreshadow at this point, is the form of psychotherapy called Cognitive Behavioral Therapy (CBT).

Anxiety

The Brain is the PLATFORM for the Mind

I often illustrate this brain/ hardware-mind/software analogy to students by asking them the following question. "If a steamroller runs over your computer what happens to the software?" (My favorite answer was the student who said, "It goes to software heaven!")

Next I ask them, tongue in cheek, "And if a steamroller runs over your head (brain) what happens to your *mind*?" Can you answer this question?

Think about it, but here is a hint. With no "platform" (neurons and neurotransmitters) to *run on*, your mind is gone, as it can't exist on a destroyed brain. Identically, your software cannot run on a crushed computer.

Let me flesh this point out because I want to show you that it leads to a much more useful understanding of anxiety and the anxiety-related disorders. And, as a result, it encourages a much more effective approach to treatment, than does the mental *illness* model. Here's why.

We know as fact that structural errors in, or damage to, your computer's hard drive have negative effects on its ability to run your software or even to work at all. A defect in manufacture, dropping your machine on the floor, pouring liquid on it and so on damage the physical bits and pieces of which it is made. If so, you need to get it repaired or buy a new one. But the second and far more likely danger to your machine is not physical but "mental"! And that is that "malware" (nasty software, such as "viruses") may be inserted into your computer's "mind" (operating system) such that the latter no longer runs as it was intended to do.

To elaborate, the problem is that while there certainly are situations in which the physical brain is not functioning properly (schizophrenia, schizoaffective disorder, the bipolar disorders, dementia, and so on), far and away the most frequently occurring mental disorders (which I noted earlier are the anxiety-related disorders) have little or nothing to do with a malfunctioning brain. It is the **mind** that has been affected and therefore the mind that must be treated ("de-bugged"). The good news is that the recently developed, talk therapy approach called Cognitive Behavioral Therapy (CBT), tailored slightly differently to each of the anxiety-related disorders, has a remarkably high success rate. This success rate, I will explain in Chapter 2, is much higher than that achieved with medication, particularly over the long run. Also, unlike medication, CBT has no negative side effects.

As I noted earlier, falling somewhere in the middle between brain dysfunctions and anxiety-related disorders in terms of frequency is Major Depressive Disorder (MDD) and its subtypes such as post-partum, seasonal and so on. MDD (known to the public as "clinical depression") is interesting because in the short run it responds equally well to anti-depressant medication (drugging the brain) and to Cognitive Behavioral Therapy (de-bugging the mind).

What is fascinating, however, is that once treatment is stopped (anti-depressant medication or CBT) those given CBT continue to maintain therapeutic gains while those who were prescribed medication are very likely to revert to their previous depressed state.

Clearly then, depression, like anxiety, is much more a mind ("mental malware") problem than a brain problem. In fact it may be the case that anti-depressants merely mask the mental pain of depression which then returns if no CBT (mental malware debugging) is concurrently provided. Some even call anti-depressants a "who cares" medication, as in, "I no longer care that I am depressed... but I am still depressed." I qualify this remark by saying that in cases of severe depression medication seems the safest course of action, in combination with CBT, of course.

Anxiety

Physical Pain / Mental Pain

Just as pain medications usually do not treat the underlying process that causes the pain, so anti-depressants do not treat the underlying mind, or "mental malware", problem. This is not to say that physical and mental pain should not be relieved. However, first and always, we should make every effort to treat the underlying cause. In other words, whether pain is physical or mental one must fix the **actual** problem and not just relieve symptoms via medication. Thus whatever "mental pain relieving medications" we may use for anxiety or depression, we still need to de-bug the mental malware (disruptive thoughts located in our mind) that is causing that distress. I will say more on this in a moment.

So where does the above discussion lead us? Let me refer to computer science once again. In another example of an analogy being both helpful but not entirely accurate, computer types break computer malware (malicious software) into categories such as "viruses", "worms" and "Trojans". For us non-computer types this hyperbolic but helpful analogy of malware as different sorts of physical entities gives us a useful way to understand the different means by which our computer can become "infected" (another analogy). But obviously we do not take it literally since dissection of the hard drive and examination under a microscope would reveal none of these three types of invaders (at least I hope not). Additionally, one does not have to don rubber gloves to work on an "infected" computer.

Thus, the analogy helps but is not literally true. Nonetheless it is helpful because we can also view each of the anxiety-related disorders as different types of **mental** malware. Malware, of course, is actually nasty computer code that disrupts your machine's software.

And what is "**mental** malware"? Well, it is darn close to the same thing, but in your mind. That is, your mind acquires, via a combination of genetic vulnerability and environmental stressors, disruptive thoughts that interfere with its smooth functioning. Drugging your brain, therefore, will not cure it. Only de-bugging your mind will remove it.

This hardware/software (brain/mind) model leads us in much better treatment directions than the mental *illness* model, with the

Anxiety

very best therapeutic approach then being an evidence-based, eclectic synthesis of biological, psychological and social treatments, each tailored to a specific mental disorder. For the anxiety-related disorders the psychological approach (via Cognitive Behavioral Therapy) must be primary, but adding "Biological" and "Social" approaches occasionally may be additionally helpful, particularly for severe forms of anxiety.

So, just as computer "malware" is not hardwired into the circuits, nor is "mental malware". Both, however, need to be de-bugged for effective use of mind or machine. Bad mental "code" (extreme anxiety, intrusive thoughts that interfere with your life, "orders" from your mind to engage in pointless or self-damaging behaviors, needless avoidance of harmless situations, and so on) **are** removable, I promise. And upon such removal, once again you will be able to "run" your life in an effective and happy fashion.

Is this really so hard to accept, that the mind is software that runs on the brain? The **brains** of adherents to different religious and political belief systems are indistinguishable from one another but their **minds** clearly are running different mental software. Could we drug such people into switching to a different belief system? No.

But "de-bugging" (changing their mind) is a possibility. Better then, to call the dysfunctional thoughts and behaviors of the anxiety-related disorders "mental malware" and to make our primary focus of treatment its removal from **the mind**. Putting this more directly, if you are suffering from an anxiety-related disorder, I do not think you are "mentally ill". Better, I would argue, to view yourself as having "picked up some mental malware" that you now need to go about de-bugging. Anxiety disorders are not brain illnesses.

Summary

In summary, in order to remove malware, that is "viruses", from your computer, physical repairs to your machine obviously will be ineffective. You need to get that malware removed. (Well, actually a complete new "mother" board could work... and wouldn't Freud be pleased to hear that!)

Similarly if you want to remove *mental* malware from your mind you will need to remove (de-bug) these disruptive thoughts. If you can afford the help of a CBT-trained psychologist as you undergo this de-bugging process so much the better but, regardless the evidence-based techniques and reference materials I will outline in this book are designed to give you all the information you need to do this on your own.

I also want to recommend you again to the website www.anxietycanada.com. You will find it an excellent resource as you move forward with tackling your particular type of anxiety. More specifically if you click on "Self-Help" and then on "Adults" and then scroll down to "Anxiety-Related Disorders" and click again you will see each of them listed and defined. Treatment strategies for each also are outlined.

In the remaining chapters of this book I will outline CBT's core features and provide you with a step-by-step approach to using it to conquer your own anxiety-related challenges. First, however, in the next chapter I will review the medications that are typically used with anxiety disorders and what the research evidence has to say about how helpful versus harmful they are.

CHAPTER **2**

MEDICATIONS FOR THE ANXIETY-RELATED DISORDERS

My hope is that the previous chapter has convinced you that the primary focus of treatment for anxiety and the anxiety-related disorders needs to be *de-bugging the mind* and not drugging the brain.

Having said that let me briefly address the harm, but occasional help, that medications can provide in the treatment of anxiety.

Biological (brain) versus Psychological (mind) Treatment Models:

I believe that two forces have led to the massive, largely ineffective, and often harmful use of medication to treat anxiety and the anxiety-related disorders.

The first of these is our "take a pill" culture. A culture heavily promoted by pharmaceutical companies across a wide range of media as well as directly to physicians via drug representatives and trade magazines. It is indeed true that safe and effective medications have been developed to assist with many physical illnesses, including brain disorders such as schizophrenia and bipolar disorder. Many lives have been improved and suffering much reduced. Researchers in these fields are to be thanked and congratulated. However, as we know, not all medications lead to significant health improvements and some make things worse.

Numerous studies show this is particularly the case for the anxiety-related disorders. The concerning fact is that some drug companies have been able to convince a number of physicians and members of the public that medicating the brain is the appropriate, frontline treatment approach for anxiety and the anxiety-related disorders.

It is not.

In North America, in particular, this marketing strategy has been especially effective and has led to significant profits for drug manufacturers. With their well-promoted claims that medication is safe and effective for anxiety, certain drug companies have seriously misled the public and the medical establishment. The facts are that in many cases these medications do more harm than good, can result in serious and long lasting side effects, and certainly should not be frontline treatment. In fact, by putting forward as "cures" numerous medications whose harms exceed their benefits, some pharmaceutical companies have very likely increased the duration of suffering for those people with anxiety-related disorders. They have also vastly increased employee absenteeism and financial costs to employers, insurers, and government.

A second reason that medication currently plays far too big a role in "treating" anxiety-related disorders, I believe, is that in North

America, insurance-covered treatment for all DSM 5 mental disorders, which includes the anxiety-related disorders, remains, almost exclusively in the hands of physicians.

Typically possessing a Bachelor's degree in one of the sciences and then going on for four years of medical training and internship, these professionals are very well prepared to handle the myriad of biological problems that can arise in the body and, of course, to refer on to specialists when appropriate. Unfortunately, unlike PhD level psychologists who spend 9-11 years studying the mind, and to a lesser extent the brain, MDs typically get only a brief exposure to psychological knowledge and treatments. Their grounding is in a biological model and that, therefore, is the approach that makes them comfortable.

Psychiatrists have more exposure to psychotherapy, and some go on to get PhDs and become researchers, but the main focus of their education also is in in the use of medications for the brain-based mental disorders. The psychological (talk therapy) part of their training, perhaps for historical reasons, often has been primarily focused on non-empirically validated "treatments", including Freudian psychoanalysis and more recent "psychodynamic" versions thereof. This said, I am pleased to note that many recent psychiatric interns are also being given some training in Cognitive Behavioral Therapy.

Further compromising their ability to enact effective psychotherapy for anxiety-related disorders is that, being MDs, the payment model for family physicians and psychiatrists typically does not make delivering CBT practical from a financial point of view. Many psychiatrists, therefore, tend to focus on mental disorders that have a significant brain illness (biological) component. Some, then, generalize this biological approach to the anxiety-related disorders despite substantial evidence showing that a psychological approach is critical to any long term recovery.

Let me stress, however, that I am not trying to over-generalize or attack a straw man. It is certainly true that many doctors and psychiatrists work closely with psychologists and some do favor a psychological approach. In fairness, it may simply be that their hands are tied when patients lack the financial resources or insurance coverage to follow through on such referrals.

Let me return to my key point. Anxiety is *not* a medical illness.

Further to this point, several of my physician friends tell me that about 30-50% of the patients they see each day actually have no biological problem at all but instead are suffering from an anxiety-related disorder – "the *worried* well", as these people are sometimes termed. Given physicians' limited training in treatment of anxiety-related disorders and pressured by a payment system in which most are reimbursed per patient visit, regardless of its length, rather than per hour (as are most psychologists) these MDs have very limited options. A quick jot on the prescription pad, therefore, becomes very tempting for keeping up with crowded waiting rooms.

Interestingly, by the way, in Great Britain, where every citizen is covered by the National Health Service (NHS), doctors are instructed to promptly refer anxiety patients directly to therapists trained in Cognitive Behavioral Therapy. Coverage for this treatment is provided under the NHS. Recently, for example, David M. Clark's *Improving Access to Psychological Services (IAPT)*, and its roll out of training high and low intensity CBT therapists placed in mental health centres throughout England, is a major move forward.

In North America some employers may provide coverage for psychological treatment. Starbucks is a notable example. Government-funded Mental Health Centers, Workers' Compensation, and automobile insurance, if appropriate, also may cover the cost of psychotherapy. Some companies also have Employee and Family Assistant Programs (EFAPs), though in my experience many of these plans provide a very limited number of sessions and often with "counsellors" (not a legally protected title) many of whom are not skilled in Cognitive Behavioral Therapy. This spotty nature of coverage for psychotherapy in North America is unfortunate because psychologist-delivered CBT, unlike medication, not only works over the short run but more importantly, treatment gains are much more likely to last over the long term due to the skills the client has acquired in the therapeutic process.

Additionally, CBT works quickly and is often best implemented *while* the employee begins a graduated return to work. This reduces absenteeism costs as well as the risk of the person developing other co-morbid ("at the same time") disorders such as Agoraphobia or Major Depressive Disorder as a consequence of being away from the social contact and structure of the workplace.

And, you may be surprised to know that actually there is no such thing as "stress leave". A physician who books an employee off work for psychological reasons is required to provide a DSM 5 diagnosis (usually one of the anxiety-related disorders or Major Depressive Disorder). "Stress leave" is not in the DSM 5 diagnostic system.

Furthermore, there is also no such thing as a "nervous breakdown". People may, on occasion, be overwhelmed by life's challenges and experience very unpleasant, *but not permanent*, symptoms. However no "nerves" are broken in either a literal or metaphoric sense. Some rest and relaxation combined with cognitive and lifestyle adjustments will usually resolve the matter. No brain illness will result.

Anxiety

The Medications

Let me now provide a more detailed discussion of what medications we are talking about and what the research has to say about their effectiveness with anxiety-related disorders.

When it comes to anxiety there are two primary categories of medications that typically are prescribed.

In very rare cases when a psychosis (loss of touch with reality) accompanies an anxiety disorder, a third category of medication, the anti-psychotics (neuroleptics) and/or "mood stabilizers" such as Lithium, also may be part of treatment, but this would be in only a tiny percentage of anxiety cases.

Benzodiazepines ("tranquil"-izers)

The first category of medications prescribed for anxiety that I will discuss is the benzodiazepines such as Valium, Xanax, Ativan and so on.

Let me ask you to reflect for a moment and think about the following questions. Do you experience extreme anxiety when you have to drive past somewhere you had an accident? Do you feel too anxious to go to social events? Find that your anxiety is lowered by repetitive mental or physical rituals? Have panic attacks? Fear going to the dentist? Have a grinding sense of being anxious almost all the time?

"No problem," say the some of the drug companies, "Just slip a Xanax under your tongue or swallow an Ativan, Valium or other tranquilizer (i.e. a benzodiazepine) and that anxiety will disappear."

Sounds good, yes? And, it even works… until it is time to pay the piper (who plays the addiction tune) a few weeks down the road when you try to stop.

Anxiety

Also, these medications cause physical impairment and are dangerous while driving a car or operating machinery. They greatly increase the risk of falls and a whole other book needs to be written about their overuse in Senior Care facilities.

Yes, there are slower acting benzodiazepines that take longer to become addicted to but the problem remains that benzodiazepines produce severe to extreme rebound anxiety if one tries to stop and thus are very hard to give up.

By way of example I am aware of a veteran school teacher who has been taking tranquilizer "crumbles" to work for 30 years (duly prescribed by his physician). Whenever the kids get to be too much he takes some. Recently this man was suddenly facing surgery which required him to stop taking his tranquilizer for some weeks prior to the operation. He went into severe withdrawal and the surgery had to be cancelled several times. Finally, and with tremendous difficulty, he was weaned from these medications.

It is important to note that benzodiazepines work on anxiety very much as does alcohol. Hence you can't take them and alcohol simultaneously. That is, they depress a part of the nervous system known as the Sympathetic ("fight/flight/freeze") Nervous System and block the adrenaline response.

Secondly, as noted above, they are highly addictive and when one runs out of pills a massive withdrawal reaction occurs. And, by the way, if you want to get someone addicted especially quickly (not that you do) prescribe these drugs "PRN" ("take one when you feel you need it").

Just as the benzodiazepines could be described as mental pain relievers, opiate medications like OxyContin, Oxycodone, Vicodin and so on, seemed to be similarly effective, but for physical rather than mental pain. Originally only recommended for extreme pain such as that caused by certain cancers, or for short term post-operative pain, some drug companies were able to convince many physicians that these drugs were also safe and effective for all sorts of non-severe, chronic pain conditions.

I think most of us now are all too aware of the still-evolving nightmare that is occurring as a consequence of addiction to these opiates. Physicians now are being pressured to stop prescribing them for other than severe pain, and insurance companies are refusing to pay for them. The consequence of this is desperately addicted people who, once cut off by their MD (who I am sure tries to wean them as gently and compassionately as possible), are going to the black market to buy their opiates and ending up accidentally over-dosing on Heroin, Fentanyl, Carfentanil, and so on.

Physicians are now beginning to experience similar pressure to be more cautious regarding their benzodiazepine (tranquilizer) prescription practices. No doubt another group of people will soon be seeking black market alternatives to these drugs and risking death in the process. You may also be interested to know that many people who have been addicted to both benzodiazepines and opiates will tell you that the benzodiazepines have even more serious withdrawal symptoms and are even more difficult to give up than opiates. When physicians finally have to turn off the opiate or benzodiazepine tap, desperate people, now deeply addicted, often risk their lives in the Russian Roulette game of street drugs.

I must emphasize three points:

First, don't give people these medications (benzodiazepines or opiates) in the first place unless absolutely needed.

Benzodiazepines, for example, may be necessary on a very short term basis for suicidal patients.

Secondly, having done so, start with a very small number of tablets. Having said that, and especially in the case of people suffering from severe pain or suicidal anxiety levels, one must never be cruel or risk patient self-harm.

"Goodness" versus "Badness" views regarding particular types of medications sometimes swing too far in an opposite direction (hormone replacement therapy after menopause is a good example) and case by case, judicious decisions must always to be made.

Thirdly, make referring anxiety sufferers for CBT the front-line treatment approach. It should be noted, by the way, that a version of CBT also helps with pain management. For those people who are already addicted to either of the above categories of drugs, careful medical weaning combined with CBT is the only compassionate path to pursue.

So why do MDs prescribe benzodiazepines? Well, I am sure that the vast majority do so reluctantly and cautiously with strict controls over the strength and number of pills. They wish to relieve mental suffering, perhaps not knowing that the "cure" often has worse consequences than the original problem. For others however, if the professional is paid per visit rather than per hour, benzodiazepines get people out of the office quickly. And, for the unscrupulous, they keep them coming back too – for the next "fix", I mean, *prescription*. The opiates and their analogues are excellent physical pain relievers and the benzodiazepines are excellent mental pain relievers. Both, however, come with a huge addiction potential and many people end up on them for life and in desperate circumstances as a result.

In conclusion, benzodiazepines, except as a very-short term emergency measure, are a very dangerous approach to treating anxiety.

In addition, and this is important, patients taking benzodiazepines rarely benefit from CBT because some anxiety, gradually introduced, is one of the keys to CBT being effective. That is, people on benzodiazepines will be unable to experience the natural rise and then drop in anxiety that the CBT steps produce, and thus no therapeutic effect may result. Patients who wish to succeed in CBT need to work in partnership with their psychologist and MD to come off benzodiazepines.

Anti-Depressants

The second category of medications that may be prescribed for the anxiety-related disorders is the anti-depressants. Originally prescribed for depression (hence the name) these medications have also shown some efficacy with anxiety. For those of you interested, among this class of medications are MAO inhibitors, Tricyclics and more recently SSRIs, SNRIs and SSNRIs. Examples would include Amitriptyline, Prozac, Effexor and Sertraline.

The hypothesis behind these medications is that they boost the length of time the neurotransmitters Serotonin, Norepinephrine and/or Dopamine remain between brain neurons. This, then, somehow may reduce depression and sometimes anxiety.

Not as addictive as the benzodiazepines, these medications seem a safer choice, though tapering off is still required.

Like all pharmaceuticals, anti-depressants have side effects. Studies show that these medications are significantly more effective than placebos for the more severe forms of the disorders discussed in this book, but usually **only when one is taking them**. Among the short term, common side effects are upset stomach, which usually resolves, plus decreased libido (sex drive), weight gain and an on-going inability to experience orgasm (especially in women).

Interestingly, their effect on retarding orgasm means they are now often prescribed for men with premature ejaculation (PE), which is an interesting example of a medication being prescribed for one of its side-effects. One might note also that there are many evidence-based and effective approaches to treating PE that do not involve medication.

One additional use for anti-depressants may be with clients for whom even the smallest of gradual exposure steps in the CBT process produces too much anxiety. Preliminary data suggest that a short term prescription for an anti-depressant (for example, Prozac) may help speed the CBT process in a limited subset of such persons, including children. CBT, however, is the key ingredient in any long term recovery.

In conclusion, the only long-term solution to mastering an anxiety-related disorder is to de-bug your mind (not drug your brain) via Cognitive Behavioral Therapy. In the next two chapters I will explain to you how to do so.

Anxiety

CHAPTER 3

ANXIETY IS THE EDGE OF PERSONAL GROWTH

Let me start this chapter with an example.

Think back to yourself as an anxious nine year old who is standing on a diving board for the first time. There you are, knees shaking, heart racing, palms sweating, and so on. Do you jump or climb down? Well maybe you did climb down a few times but eventually many of you stood there and… jumped!

"Wow," you thought, "that was pretty amazing, *and* I am still alive!"

Had you not vastly over-estimated the risk of harm? Were your friends/parents proud of you? Did you not go up a hundred times more and graduate to cannon balls and dives?

Should your mom have run up the ladder and slipped a Xanax under your tongue or given you an Ativan? Hardly!

Here is my central point. At extreme levels there is no question that anxiety is highly unpleasant. However, at a moderate to mid-high level, **anxiety is pre-requisite to personal growth.** And, as I will discuss in Chapter 6, it is also a pre-requisite for a fulfilling and joyful life-well-lived – a life that you can look back on in your 80s or 90s and think, "Hey, I made a fool of myself a few times but overall, wow, I really LIVED my life!"

You may have read that the only difference between a hero and a coward is that, while both are afraid, a hero does it anyway. "Doing it anyway" is exactly what is required to resolve your anxiety, and anxiety-related disorders, but in a *baby steps* fashion, of course. Nobody is asking you to start on the ten meter diving board.

Anxiety

Working against your acceptance of a *baby steps of courage* solution to your anxiety challenges are elements within the prescription drug industry which, as noted earlier, seems to have made it their goal to convince society that anxiety is a medical illness and most effectively treated via medication.

My contention, on the other hand, is that anxiety is **not** an illness and it rarely requires medication. Mastering it requires guided courage not drugs. Such courage is enacted systematically and step by step and is not a leap of faith!

Metaphorically, how about start by just sliding into the water into a loved one's arms, as a little boy might bravely do into his mother's. Meanwhile his big sister already loves the diving board as, no doubt, will he in a few years, after following her sequence of anxiety and growth-producing baby steps.

The Pros and Cons of Anxiety

So what is ANXIETY?

Anxiety is part of the evolutionarily adaptive *fight, flight or freeze* response. It can save your life in a physical emergency but it can also bully you into leading a more and more limited, and even bizarre, existence.

Importantly, and this is key: facing anxiety and noting the *actual* rather than imagined consequences, is the beginning of personal growth.

That doesn't mean it is necessarily pleasant, though it can be. Think of exciting movies, skiing, bicycling, rollercoaster riding, zip lining, and so on – all fun because they produce anxiety. Think also of the toast to the bride you agreed to give. Sure you may have died a thousand deaths beforehand, but after all, it was about her not you, and when you got your first laugh was it not all worthwhile? And when the tearful bride came up later and hugged you, weren't you glad you stepped up? Not convinced yet? Well keep reading.

Anxiety

Anxiety as Friend

Let's start by discussing anxiety as your friend. In a physical emergency, by activating a number of body systems that increase your breathing, heart rate, strength and so on, the anxiety/fight-or-flight response can save your life.

However, as we all know, while adaptive in physical emergencies, this response also may be activated when you don't want or need it. It may trigger in situations where it does more harm than good. This is because your mind often can't tell the difference between a genuine physical emergency and a psychological, or false, "emergency". As noted above, changes like an increase in heart rate and breathing (to give more oxygen to muscles so you can run or fight), an increase in pupil size (so you can see better), increased sweating (to keep you cool), shutting down digestion (to help send more blood to your muscles), and so on all help promote survival in physical emergencies. In psychologically stressful situations, however, these bodily changes are the last thing you want or need.

Anxiety as Your Enemy

The problem is that your mind (which, as you now know, is the *software* that runs on your brain) often cannot tell the difference between when these responses are adaptive and when they are not. It may incorrectly direct the brain to enact the fight/flight/freeze response when it does harm, not good. A misinterpretation by your mind may tell your body to activate the fight/flight/freeze reaction in response to events or thoughts that are not actually dangerous. The sad consequence of this is that rather than you getting braver and more competent, instead, your world may shrink and your time be wasted in pointless worrying, avoidance, and in time-wasting, ineffective rituals.

Let me elaborate. Hyperventilating is great when running from a sabre-toothed tiger, but it is the "gasoline on the fire" in a panic attack. Sweating is great for staying cool when fighting or fleeing, but downright embarrassing when you are speaking to a crowd (and let's not even mention what happens to your bowels under stress).

In these situations, your mind, as it does in physical emergencies, tells your brain (specifically the HPA or, hypothalamic-pituitary-

Anxiety

adrenal axis), to direct your body to activate your emergency response. Your body then releases several hormones (adrenaline, also known as epinephrine, and others) that cause the physical changes mentioned above. The result is the triggering of extreme and highly unpleasant anxiety.

In a physical emergency stress hormones are quickly burned off via running or fighting. In a psychological "emergency" however, they make it very difficult for you to take adaptive action. Additionally they linger, perhaps for hours, coursing through your bloodstream doing damage via the blood clotting compound they release as well as by raising your blood pressure. Worse, they cause you considerable suffering in situations where such responses only defeat your best intentions and interests. Over time they create a self-imposed prison and try to force you to live in it.

Two Brains / Two Minds

Interestingly, when the mind tells the brain to respond to danger, real or perceived, you really are very much of two minds. The response runs on two distinct brain areas.

As a quick but related aside, when people say something like, "I am schizophrenic about this," meaning, they think, "I am of two minds," they are misusing the word schizophrenic. Schizophrenia is a brain illness which affects the functioning of the mind, in which one is *split from reality*. It is not a state of being of two minds or having a "split personality". In fact (perhaps this is more than you want to know) a better analogy would be for indecisive people to say they are suffering from Dissociative Identity Disorder, which used to be called Multiple Personality Disorder – another DSM 5 disorder (not covered in this book) that you might enjoy reading up on.

Anyway (forgive this professor – we tend to wander) when I say *you are of two minds* with each running on a different area of the brain platform, what I mean is that in certain very high stress situations two different parts of your mind, and the respective

Anxiety

brain areas on which they operate, may draw very different conclusions about the meaning of an event.

Take for example a person who has acquired a phobia to driving and/or PTSD as the result of a car accident. I handled many such cases in my private practice.

There they are, driving along minding their own business when suddenly they are T-boned by an inattentive driver who missed a stop sign. Physical injuries aside, such people may well develop the anxiety-related disorder called Specific Phobia (to driving) and/or Post Traumatic Stress Disorder. These disorders may be so strong that the person feels too stressed to be willing to get into a car again or too terrified to drive near the accident site, since to do so causes a massively unpleasant fight/flight/ freeze response. This response may so strong that it imprisons them.

"Why," they ask me, "is this happening? My spouse tells me I am being silly, that it was a fluke accident and won't occur again. AND I AGREE! So how come, Doc, I am a mess when I look at my car, try get in my car, or try to drive near the accident spot?"

Here is the reason. The part of your mind which runs on the pre-frontal cortex, just above your eyebrows, is saying, correctly, "It was a freak situation. I am perfectly safe, so there is no need to activate the fight/flight/freeze response when I want to drive, or drive near, where the accident occurred."

However, a second part of your mind, running on another brain area called the amygdala, which specializes in learning dangers, amongst other duties, is saying, "There is no way you are EVER again getting in that death machine and/or driving near the site of the accident! And if you try to, I will fill you with so much adrenaline that you will feel absolutely awful."

And this amygdala part of your mind, by the way, has a much longer evolutionary history in human heads than does your cerebral cortex and often wins the argument. Thus you are of two minds: one that says, "Don't be silly, get back to normal driving." And a second that says, "No way! Driving, especially near the site, is fatally dangerous."

Cognitive Behavioral Therapy

It is Cognitive Behavioral Therapy (CBT) that will resolve the conflict between the two conclusions your mind has drawn – "safe" versus "dangerous".

Yes, you are being *silly* from your logical, cognitive mind's point of view, but for many people the amygdala overpowers the pre-frontal cortex and thus they *can't* (see Chapter 6 for a discussion of "can't" versus "won't") return to normal driving. The amygdala does help you remember legitimate dangers, so it does appear to be helpful but not always. Given that your non-rational amygdala mind is currently winning, what can you do?

The answer is twofold. On the one hand, you have to desensitize your amygdala and get it to stop stimulating the fight or flight adrenaline response when there is no need to do so. You do this via step by step behavioral (B) exposure to the situation you fear.

Secondly, and simultaneously, you have to strengthen that cognitive (C) part of your mind running on the pre-frontal cortex so it can override the incorrectly catastrophic conclusions your amygdala has drawn. You do this by plucking up your courage and taking step-by-step Behavioral risks. The consequences of those actions are then analysed by your cognitive, frontal lobes who note that actually *nothing* bad happened. Now that you know that reality, you can update your inaccurate fear of imminent danger and instead realize that, actually there is no danger. You can then go on to the next behavioral risk, observe that it too was safe, then change your dangerousness assessment, and so on. It is the back and forth between these "C" and "B" techniques that are the essence of Cognitive Behavioral Therapy (CBT).

Fear Ladders

And more specifically how do you do this? Let me foreshadow the next chapter on CBT for a moment.

First, you need to build a "fear ladder" in which you write down, from bottom to top (easiest to hardest) a series of increasingly difficult steps that you need to master to be able to return to a normal driving life. Each step on the ladder needs to provoke significant anxiety but not so much that you can't **remain** in the situation, and let that anxiety wash over you until it drops to a normal range. If the anxiety you deliberately (bravely) provoke is too high and you escape, you will only be strengthening that anxiety's hold over you via your escape/avoidance.

For some of you that first step will be very small but this is fine as long as it gets you to at least a 7/10 zone of anxiety (psychologists call these numbers SUDs or subjective units of discomfort). You then deliberately put yourself in the first situation (the one near the bottom of the ladder that you feel you can do and not have to escape from) and calmly **wait** (perhaps doing some slow "in through the nose out through the mouth" breathing) until your anxiety drops to a 2 or 3 out of 10. **And it will.**

You then keep repeating that step until you feel ready to move to ladder step #2. The size of these steps should be big enough to make the next one provoke at least a 7/10 on your anxiety scale but not so high that you can't stay in it and wait out your feelings. You then keep moving up our fear ladder rung by rung until your amygdala (metaphorically) says, "Okay, I'm sorry. I will let you drive normally again." And the frontal lobes say, "I told you so!"

Note also that in your mind (cognitively) you should focus on how your "disaster" expectations in each step are proving not to be true as you move forward with the exposure process. In reality you are not "going crazy" (you can't, by the way); are not "about to die"; are not "losing your mind"; and so on.

In fact, despite the temporary, unpleasant sensations, actually you are **just fine**. Having enacted this process with many, many clients (first in my office, next in my car, and finally in their car with them driving) this process works and, in fact, you can do it on your own. This is why I say that anxiety truly is the edge of personal growth, in life in general, and certainly when you are resolving an anxiety-related disorder.

Anxiety

Avoidance Strengthens Anxiety

To conclude this chapter I want you to think hard about whether anxiety is really something you want to avoid? Sometimes life, plus some inherited psychological vulnerabilities, puts us in situations that will indeed activate an extreme anxiety response. That is just how it goes.

An accident can leave you with mental malware like a Phobia or PTSD. A tendency to be over sensitive to your bodily sensations can lead to Panic Disorder. An inherited shy nature can leave you open to developing Social Anxiety Disorder. Too much time at home can lead to Agoraphobia, and so on. Each of these circumstances, unfortunately, may cause you to experience a specific form of extreme anxiety reaction even though this reaction is not only unnecessary, it is hugely counterproductive. The good news is that there is a proven way to manage, then shrink and often eliminate, such reactions so you can get back to a full and happy life.

Finally, I want you to remember the title of this chapter is "Anxiety is the Edge of Personal Growth". And I want you to consider that many of experiences in your life that caused you to grow as a person were preceded or accompanied by anxiety. Was it not those "anxious moments" that caused you to grow and develop your personality and competence, first as a child and now as an adult? Don't trade that courage and growth for the prison of medication and avoidance. Instead, walk with me through the next chapter and I can promise you that the behavioral "sensible risks" and cognitive analysis I am going to ask you to undertake will open those prison doors and allow you to return to a life as a self-actualizing and growing person.

In the next chapter, I will show you how to use CBT to undo the anxiety-related disorders that may be plaguing you. Yes, doing so will require you to put your anxiety into the 7/10 range for short periods of time. But, given the huge benefits that will result, isn't seeing anxiety as an opportunity for growth a vastly more helpful thought to carry with you through life than is constantly dreading and avoiding it? Let alone drugging it away?

Anxiety

In my view, anxiety is *not* a mental "illness" or any sort of illness at all. It is instead some "mental malware" that you have picked up through no fault of your own. Debugging it is surprisingly straight forward.

CHAPTER 4

COGNITIVE BEHAVIORAL THERAPY

Let me begin this chapter with a brief description of how one acquires one or more of the nine anxiety types that are the subject of this book. This will then lead into a discussion of the core techniques for de-bugging them.

Anxiety via Associations

The first factor that can lead you developing an anxiety-related disorder is called Associative Learning. This process, also called Classical or Pavlovian conditioning, was first described by the Russian physiologist, Ivan Pavlov. Let me give you an example.

Let's say you get into an elevator. Pavlov would call the elevator a "neutral stimulus" because it currently causes no particular response within you. It is benign, no big deal. But then let's say that just after the door closes you hear an extremely loud "Bang" sound which frightens you. This sudden noise will then automatically activate your emergency, "fight/flight/freeze", response. In Pavlovian terms the noise is called an "unconditioned stimulus" because loud noises automatically produce a startle and fear response in you. Your fear reaction to this stimulus he called an "unconditioned response" because no "conditioning" or training is required. The response happens automatically.

Key here is that because the fight/flight/freeze response happens **while** you are in an elevator your mind (aided by your brain which directs the body to release adrenaline and other hormones and neurotransmitters) is likely to automatically associate the two. In Pavlov's terms you have now become "conditioned" to respond to elevators with extreme fear. The elevator, which previously was a "neutral stimulus" (no big deal), has now become a "conditioned stimulus" and it leads, automatically, to the "conditioned response" of terror. You now have a phobia (irrationally strong fear) of elevators rooted, in your amygdala.

Let me make this point more simply.

Sometimes anxiety-related disorders are learned by association. Something that genuinely frightens or terrifies you gets attached to something that didn't bother you previously. This new thing or situation now causes you extreme fear. Let me refer you back to my car example in Chapter 3. Getting hit by another car while you are driving naturally frightens you badly which then can cause the creation of an automatic fight/flight/freeze reaction to driving, especially near the accident scene. This newly acquired, conditioned fear response (this "mental malware") then makes it very distressing or, "impossible" for you to enter your car, or perhaps to drive by the accident location without an extremely unpleasant anxiety response.

There are many examples of this. Children think puppies are cute but if they are bitten by one then the previously neutral (or even positive) stimulus "puppy" will now evoke an extreme fear response. This fear then may generalize to all dogs.

Anxiety

As an interesting example, I recall a student who told me she had a life-long fear of balloons as a result of one unexpectedly popping in her face at her fifth birthday party. Similarly, and more seriously, a site where you are assaulted becomes associated with the terror you felt during the incident and you now avoid that location because of the highly upsetting, adrenaline/terror response it has come to trigger. Associative learning plays a large role in many of the anxiety-related disorders and at least a partial role in all of them. As I will explain shortly it also holds the key to a powerful debugging tool.

Anxiety via Role Models

A second factor that can lead to the development of an anxiety-related disorder occurs via what psychologists, such as Albert Bandura, call "modelling" or Social Learning. Social Learning theory says we learn some of our irrational fears (remember, an anxiety-related disorder is a fear of something far in excess of what is actually necessary) via role-modelling from our parents and others.

I recall, for example, that my mother had a terrible fear of spiders. There were no dangerous spiders where she grew up nor are there any where I live. This phobia was passed on to me via her modelling of how much they scared her. Fortunately, though, because I am a psychologist I fixed myself up later, using CBT of course! The lesson from this is to keep your irrational fears to yourself. Don't pass them on to your children.

Anxiety via Negative Reinforcement (Avoidance)

Given that you now have acquired an anxiety-related disorder a third mechanism then kicks in which ingrains it more deeply. What happens is that you begin to avoid the location or memories (thoughts) of the events that caused your original anxiety response because they reactivate it so severely. Because of the highly unpleasant, adrenaline-flooding reaction such locations and memories provoke, you desperately try to stay away from them, either physically, or by distracting yourself mentally (via distraction or "dissociation").

One spin-off of this, as happens in Obsessive-Compulsive Disorder, is that you may engage in reassuring but time consuming mental or physical rituals in order to distract and reassure yourself, in an effort to avoid your anxiety. Hoarding and Body-Focussed Repetitive Disorder (for example, skin picking or eyebrow plucking) provide similar, self-damaging distractions. Psychologists call these techniques "avoidance".

Critically, **avoidance is precisely what stops people from being able to de-bug mental malware.**

In our example above, for instance, after your big elevator scare you now avoid them (or dogs, or balloons, or where you had a crash, or where you saw someone killed, or traumatic memories, and so on).

The huge problem, however, is that your avoidance reinforces (strengthens) the fear. It does this by rewarding you with a reduction in fear (removing something unpleasant is reinforcing and is called negative reinforcement) because you can't get upset by these memories or locations if you physically and/or mentally avoid them.

Tragically, however, this is where you then pay the awful price of an ever-shrinking world filled with more and more internal and external triggers for your anxiety. The result is that you become increasingly imprisoned by the false "need" to enact ever more damaging, costly and time wasting rituals to avoid facing your fear. An anxiety-related disorder, be it PTSD, Social Anxiety Disorder, OCD or any of the others is only conquerable by facing it.

Anxiety

My point here is that physical or mental avoidance **maintains and strengthens** an anxiety-related disorder. Note also that anti-anxiety medications such as Xanax, Ativan and the other benzodiazepines, as well as alcohol, do the same thing. They provide temporary relief, at the huge cost of addiction, by blocking your adrenaline response and allowing you to avoid the discomfort produced by the things or thoughts you currently fear. This, of course, then deepens and hardens your anxiety-related disorder.

Psychologists John Watson and B.F. Skinner are well known for having shown that positive reinforcement strengthens behaviors – desirable ones and undesirable ones, by the way. Reward a child for being kind and you will get more kindness. Reward (give in to) a whiny child and you will get more whining.

For purposes of this discussion, however, much more important is Skinner's other discovery that not only does positive reinforcement strengthen behaviors but, as noted above, so does **negative reinforcement**. It is important to note that negative reinforcement is **not** punishment. Punishment is the application of something unpleasant. Negative reinforcement is the **removal** of something unpleasant and it reinforces behaviors just as strongly as does positive reinforcement. People find it rewarding when something unpleasant is removed. Therefore if you remove anxiety by avoiding a triggering location or thought then you are reinforcing (strengthening) that anxiety, thus making it worse. Anxiety can be a bully and if you feed that bully by avoiding what you fear – even though this is a natural thing to do – or by drugging away your fear response, then that bully will grow stronger and stronger. Instead you need to develop and enact a careful plan to push back against it and exile it from your life and mind.

Avoidance, then, is the key factor in maintaining rather than conquering an anxiety-related disorder.

You need to stop doing it. Not all at once but, as I said in Chapter 3, via a carefully planned, step-by-step process. That process also needs to be tailored slightly differently to each person and to their particular anxiety-related disorder.

Anxiety via Thinking Errors

The fourth factor in acquiring and maintaining an anxiety-related disorder is thinking (cognitive) errors.

You may recall the saying, "As we *think* so shall we *feel.*" Your thoughts and behaviors lead to predicable emotions. So why not choose those thoughts and behaviors that are to your advantage?

Let me give you a personal example. Later today I am booked to chair a debate in front of 300 people. Should I allow my self-talk to be, "What if I make a fool of myself?" "What if I forget a key step in the debate sequence?" "What if…what if…what if…?"

Absolutely not, as catastrophic thinking will only increase my anxiety and worsen my performance. Instead my self-talk is, "This is going to be fun." "It is not about me but about the topic." "Even if I make a few mistakes I know the audience will benefit from this event," and so on.

Many people have the strange idea that they are a victim of their mind. But it is *your* mind (it is you!) and you can train yourself to manage it as you wish. It just takes practice. "What If-ing", vastly over-estimating danger, and catastrophic thinking need to be examined for their inaccuracy and firmly banished from your mind.

Further to this you will recall the old joke in which a person goes to a doctor, bends their elbow and says to the doctor, "Doctor, it hurts when I do that." And the doctor says… I bet you know: "Don't do that."

So how about this? A client goes to a psychologist and says, "Doc, it hurts when I think that." And the psychologist says, you know, yes? "Then don't think that!"

A critical part of the "C" (cognitive) part of CBT is to remember that it is **your** mind and you actually can learn to use it to shrink and eliminate the anxiety bullies (mental malware) that are currently spoiling your full enjoyment of life.

Anxiety Levels: 1-10

I am now going to explain to you about anxiety levels and how, by tuning in to yours, you can learn to back off your anxiety "bullies". This is best done via a subjective measurement system psychologists call *Selective Units of Discomfort* or *SUDs.*

SUDs vary from 1-10 and are your personal, internal assessment of how uncomfortable certain thoughts or behaviors make you. They are your personal assessment of how much discomfort you are experiencing at any given moment.

Anxiety, thus your current SUD level, up to about a 4 or 5 out of 10 is tolerable, even fun. And in fact it can play a positive role by motivating us, as well as by helping us to grow as a person. It motivated me to make sure I was fully prepared for my debate. Anxiety at a 9 or 10 out of 10, however, evokes the highly unpleasant fight/flight/freeze response and, barring massive courage on our part, may block us from doing what we need to do. If you have an anxiety-related disorder then it is very likely that the strength of your anxiety response is at that 9 or 10 out of 10 level. If your anxiety is at an 8/10 you may not qualify for an official diagnosis but you are still suffering. Having an anxiety-related problem in the 8/10 to 10/10 range is, to say the least, no fun. So our goal here is not to eliminate all anxiety (lest we not grow as a person) but rather to take those circumstances when it gets intolerably high and learn to back it off to a more reasonable level. This we do in a carefully planned, step-by-step fashion.

CBT

So, knowing the four mechanisms for acquiring and maintaining anxiety disorders how do we de-bug them?

We do so through a combination of Cognitive (mental) and Behavioral (real world) techniques, hence the term Cognitive Behavioral Therapy.

In my own professional experience some of my clients have responded better to the "B" or Behavioral techniques of CBT (change what you **do**) while others gained more from the "C" or Cognitive approaches (change what you **think**). But all clients require some of both.

Your goal in taking on anxiety or an anxiety-related disorder is to get your acquired automatic anxiety response to certain thoughts, feelings, things or places *to back off* so that you can begin to live a more normal life.

Please remember, though, that this does *not* mean that you want to live a life without anxiety. Remember, "anxiety is the edge of personal growth". But you do want to live without that anxiety staying at or close to the level of a DSM 5 mental disorder. The one deal we are going to have to make here is that to bring about the drop in anxiety level you seek, I am going to ask you to be brave and to tolerate putting yourself into some 7/10 anxiety situations.

Allow me to elaborate.

Exposure

As I foreshadowed in Chapter 3 the first thing in resolving your anxiety-related disorder is to set up what psychologists call a "fear ladder". That is a "ladder" with each rung a little to harder to do than the one below it. That ladder might be about becoming more comfortable around people, or being able to ride elevators, or being able to handle memories of a tragic event, or to not over-react to bodily sensations that can trigger a panic attack, or backing off some of your reassurance rituals, and so on. Let's start with a simple example and talk about how to eliminate a phobia (irrational fear) of elevators. Keep in mind, however, that the core principles for how to do so also apply across all the anxiety-related disorders. In Part II of this book I will provide additional detail in how to apply CBT to your particular anxiety type as well as refer you to additional resources.

Okay, so let's get specific about this "fear ladder" approach to our elevator phobia. Step 1 is to take a piece of paper and draw a big ladder on it with wide rungs spaced far enough apart to allow room for you to write. At the very top of this ladder you might write "Being able to ride in an elevator for 15 or more floors without my distress rising above a 3/10 level". A rung below that might be riding less than five floors also at a 3/10, and below that riding one floor. Lower still would be pushing the elevator button and letting the doors open but not getting in. Lower still, could be walking past an elevator. Below that might be seeing an elevator down the hall and below that perhaps looking at pictures of elevators on the internet. Next you need to select a "rung" on the ladder that evokes a significant but not intolerable anxiety response within you. Key here is that the step is not so anxiety-producing ("get me out of here") that you won't be able to remain in that situation ("tough it out") until your anxiety drops (it will). If you do escape then you need to try a lower rung.

These steps are what psychologists call the "in vivo" (in real life) part of our plan. Yes, the exposure will distress you (perhaps to a 7/10 level or a bit higher) but it won't harm you and, I promise, your anxiety response will soon drop below that number if you simply, regardless of your bodily sensations and catastrophic thoughts, remain in the situation.

Now, if the bottom rung of this behavioral ladder turns out to be too anxiety-producing (you can't make yourself do it or, if you do try it, you escape before your anxiety has a chance to drop) then try some other, even easier steps below in which you simply *imagine* yourself in a series of increasingly challenging elevator-related situations. These "imaginal" steps do not require you to <u>do</u> any of the above behaviors but rather each step is simply imagined in your mind and you stay with that thought until your anxiety drops. This, psychologists call, "imaginal exposure". The imaginal steps might be the same as the real life ("in vivo") ones but all we do is think about each of them, one at a time, from easiest to hardest. The process is the same. We start at the bottom and **think** about seeing an elevator down the hall. This raises our anxiety and we simply wait until our anxiety no longer rises above a 2-3 out of 10. We then start mentally "moving up the ladder" making certain that we linger on each step enough times that it no longer increases our anxiety to more than a two to three out of ten before we go up to the next step.

Anxiety Drops Naturally

Key to the above, we are going to take advantage of a correct but little known thing about the anxiety response and that is if you do **nothing** it will drop all by itself. This seems remarkable but it is absolutely true.

In other words if you are willing to *place* yourself in a situation (or, if you are not ready for that, then *imagine* yourself in a situation) relating to your particular anxiety-related disorder that puts you to at least a 7/10 on your personal anxiety scale, and then just **wait it out** and not distract yourself, I promise you your anxiety will fall to a 2-3/10 within a few minutes.

No need to be too brave here, though it won't harm you to do so as long whatever anxiety level you choose to face is one you can "stay with" until it drops and stays dropped. It just mustn't be one you run away from. Higher than 7/10 is fine but if it is too high then escaping the situation before your anxiety drops naturally will only strengthen your anxiety. So pick a level for which you can "hang in there". While doing an exposure step just let the anxiety response wash over you and *wait...*

Anxiety

While you are doing this waiting I am going to ask you to be "mindful", that is, to focus on being in the present, feeling whatever you feel, and to not distract yourself with thoughts about the past or future. Considerable recent data shows that experiencing the anxiety and staying "in the present" as it washes over you is a central technique for reducing such anxiety over the long term. This approach is also a good overall anxiety reduction technique in everyday life. In other words just let the anxiety "be", and then pass, rather than getting upset about it.

Control Your Thoughts

Thirdly, and this is also very powerful, I am going to ask you to take control of your cognitions (thoughts) during the exposure process and muster them to your advantage rather than let them make things worse. Catastrophic thoughts are where the anxiety cascade begins and must be stopped immediately. **Don't let them even get started** and if they do start then shut them down right away.

I am sure you can guess what *helpful* versus *harmful* thoughts might be in this situation. "I am going to die" (or versions thereof) is not one of them! Challenging such thoughts is critical. For example, "I am going to die," might be challenged with, "But I am not dead, am I, so stop lying to me, silly mind." Or, "Do I know anyone who has ever been hurt in an elevator crash?" Or, "How many people a year are killed by elevator failures?"

This challenging of inaccurately catastrophic cognitions, in each of the nine anxiety-related disorders, is the key to the cognitive part of CBT. If you hear yourself thinking catastrophic thoughts firmly challenge the evidence that they are true and then banish them from your mind.

Anxiety

Comparing your fears to the actual evidence of what happens during each behavioral exposure step is central to beating any anxiety-related disorder.

Don't Hyperventilate

The fourth thing we will take advantage of is that we know that anxiety is increased by gulping air through our mouths. Hyperventilating is a natural part of the fight/flight/freeze response and very helpful in a physical emergency because you need the extra oxygen.

However, in a psychological "emergency", it is like throwing gasoline on a fire and leads to very unpleasant, heart attack-like sensations which only further upset you. Therefore, as you begin to enact Step 1 on your fear ladder, and for each subsequent step, I ask you to breathe in through your nose only (to limit oxygen intake) and to breathe out through your mouth (to clear excess carbon dioxide). This management of your oxygen/carbon dioxide balance is a key component of managing your anxiety response.

Progressive Muscle Relaxation

Finally, some of you may find it helpful to engage in what is called "progressive muscle relaxation" before you begin to climb the ladder.

When we are anxious we tend to hold our muscles tighter than is necessary and this can lead to anxiety headaches, neck and shoulder pain and so on. While we could just train ourselves to work through each muscle group (toes up to head works best), and consciously relax each muscle area, what is more effective is, instead, to deliberately tighten each muscle group (starting with your toes) as tight as you can for a count of eight seconds, and then let it relax fully. This will allow tension in those muscles to drop significantly lower than simply relaxing the area. Working up the body from toes to calves to thighs to stomach to neck to face (scrunch it up) is an excellent way to drop anxiety. And to fall asleep too, by the way.

Applying the Anxiety Reduction Principles

Alright, so we now have six things going for us.

Three behavioral techniques:

- Progressive muscle relaxation before we start

- Brave exposure steps, and

- Not hyperventilating,

Plus, three cognitive techniques:

- Calmly waiting once we have taken a brave step until our anxiety drops to a 3/10

- Not catastrophizing, and

- Noting that nothing bad is actually happening during each step.

So, should we start with our imaginal or our behavioral (real world) ladder? Well, let's say that we just aren't ready for the behavioral steps yet.

Let's try **Step 1** on our lower (imaginary) ladder: We imagine an elevator in our mind and we **wait**. No distracting ourselves and certainly no Ativan, Xanax and so on. You will recall in Chapter 2 that I stated that benzodiazepines wreck CBT because your anxiety can't get to the required minimum 7/10 level. Also, we breathe in through the nose and out through the mouth so we can't hyperventilate. Finally we challenge catastrophic thoughts, note that our fears are not actually happening and keep our cognitions positive. We may also engage in progressive muscle relaxation just before we deliberately trigger a planned ladder step.

And guess what happens if we just *wait*? Our anxiety will begin to drop. Seven, six, five, four, three... maybe two. Great!

Okay, let's do it again... Hmmm, drops even faster... Again... Wow, didn't even go to a 5 at the start and dropped instantly. Do it again... and again. You will know you have spent enough time on each step when after going through it several times you will now be saying to yourself, "This is boring."

Excellent! Boring sure is not anxious, correct? Now you are ready to move up a step.

Okay, **Step 2**. Now we are going to imagine pushing the button and the door opening.

"Yikes," it went up to 8 when you imagined that. It's okay. Just wait…wait…wait... and **down** goes the anxiety.

Do it again… drops faster… Do it again… and again until you get to… boring. Add some helpful catastrophe-challenging thoughts.

On to **Step 3**. This time we are going to picture getting in the elevator and going up one floor. Once again, "Yikes" but just wait, wait, wait, and your anxiety will drop.

Then do it again, again and again until you are now bored with this process.

Okay, time to imagine the five floor ride and, when you can do that comfortably you can move to the top of the ladder and imagine the big 15 floor ride.

Well Done!

Alright, if you can now do the imaginal phase of treatment with none of the steps putting you above a 3/10, you are ready to begin the in vivo (real life), exposure steps – and by all means start with the behavioral ladder if you can. Again we don't want to rush things as if we don't fully master (get bored with) each step, this won't work.

Okay here we go.

For **Step 1** we look up images of elevators on the internet. We do our muscle relaxation and then look at the picture, remembering to breathe in only through nose, not to distract ourselves, and to keep useful cognitions in our mind ("Big deal, it is an elevator"). Then we wait and sure enough, our anxiety drops. We then repeat this step until it no longer prompts an anxiety response beyond a 3/10.

Now we move on to **Step 2** where we must go to a building with an elevator and look at it from down the hall.

Same thing.

Then the *push-the-button-but-don't-get-in* step, then a one floor ride, five floor ride, and finally 15 floors. In each step we must wait until our anxiety drops and repeat that step until it is no big deal. Ho-hum, another ride on the elevator!

How many rungs should you do per day? How quickly should you "climb"?

Well it is up to you but just be sure to not move up to the next "rung" until you are fully desensitized to (bored by) the one you are currently working on.

"Sure," you say, "this is pretty easy with the elevator example but what about my panic attacks, my horrible PTSD memories, my terror of not doing my OCD rituals, my terror of leaving the house and so on?"

Trust me here – the same core principles apply. One step at a time, you need to tackle your feared thoughts, memories, sensations or behaviors and then work your way up your fear ladder.

As I said earlier, avoidance reinforces fears because it temporarily reduces anxiety, as do anti-anxiety drugs.

Procrastination works the same way. "Oh no, I have a report due in two weeks," you think. "Oh well, I will start on it tomorrow." While this avoidance may temporarily drop your anxiety, what it then does is increase your anxiety the next day. The trouble of course is that each avoidance cranks the underlying anxiety higher. Had you got on with your deadlined task today when your anxiety may have been about a 5/10, you likely would have been productive. But tomorrow it will be at a 6/10 and pretty soon it will be too high for you to function effectively. And when it is 9/10 the night before your report is due, is writing it then going to be easy? Be fun? Not a chance, because writing papers when one is in a 9/10 anxiety state is highly unpleasant at the least, and impossible at the worst. Impossible because the fight/flight/freeze response is cranked to the maximum.

Further tripping you up is the additional truth that when anxiety is high one has a narrowed focus of attention, making complex tasks even harder. Interestingly and sadly, virtually all of the plagiarized papers I have received from students over the years were "written" the night before the paper was due. Start early.

In this chapter I have stressed that CBT is "evidence-based". In the next chapter I will elaborate on what this means and give you some skills to ascertain if a therapy you are considering meets this criterion.

CHAPTER 5

THE CASE FOR EVIDENCE-BASED TREATMENT

Science versus Quackery

In this chapter I will elaborate on why I believe it is important to make therapy decisions on the basis of scientific research.

While "pop psychology" ("popularized" psychology without any scientific backing) sometimes may be entertaining, its track record for successfully treating anxiety-related disorders is dismal. It seems like every month another "therapy" appears in the popular press and is supposedly a "breakthrough" for curing what ails you. Quackery has a long history: a long history of failure, except for its practitioners who often acquire significant wealth. As PT

Anxiety

Barnum is reputed to have said, "There is a sucker born every minute," and I think this is more like every ten seconds on the fringes of my own field. Some of these "therapies" are quite amusing, some dangerous, but all are a con.

Let me tell you how I look at all this. I suspect that if you were suddenly suffering from acute appendicitis you would definitely seek out a scientifically valid treatment and a scientifically trained treatment provider. You are going to place your bet on a skilled surgeon who, using the latest, evidence-based techniques (which get better every year thanks to on-going research), is far more likely to save your life than will going "gluten-free", getting "re-birthed", or having a Shaman chant for you.

I am asking in this chapter that you consider applying similar, critical thinking ("Fact Checking") to your psychotherapy choices. In other words when you are in serious trouble you don't mess around. You go for the best.

Just as surgeons, oncologists, obstetricians and other medical specialists continue to become increasingly skilled at dealing with many previously fatal or debilitating conditions, CBT psychologists (who also must base their treatment methods on ever-advancing, evidence-based research) similarly have developed very effective techniques.

This is particularly true when it comes to de-bugging the mental malware that causes the anxiety-related disorders. So, yes there are people out there that will say they have effective "alternative" treatments for anxiety.

"Fine," I say but, "show me the evidence." And it had better be from reputable sources and replicated by other independent researchers.

Spontaneous Remission

So what do I mean by "evidence-based"?

There are three broad categories of reasons why people get better, be it from a physical or a mental disorder.

One is the passage of time. Some disorders just go away. People with sore backs or depression, for example, often show improvement simply by doing nothing and letting time pass. This is called "spontaneous remission". Spontaneous remission occurs for some physical and for some mental disorders, but clearly not all. And, by the way, if someone swung a dead chicken over your head *while* spontaneous remission was occurring, was it the chicken? Or whatever other type of quackery ("cluckery"?!) that was being performed at the same time?

When it comes to the anxiety-related disorders the data unfortunately are clear that these disorders rarely remit (go away) spontaneously. Instead, they require effective treatment.

Placebos

A second reason people may improve is due to the so-called placebo effect (from the Latin "I shall please").

Let's say our sufferers go to see a "professional" with a nice office, some sort of degrees on the wall, smartly dressed, and so on. Sometimes, even if that "professional" provides no valid treatment, the client's **belief** that the person is competent to help them leads to some improvement.

I assume your mother's lips did not contain a local anesthetic but nonetheless her "kissing it better" often helped. The placebo effect is especially powerful if a pill (sugar pill or, more recently, a "miracle supplement") is provided. Further to this latter point, my pet peeve is those supplements that say they "support brain health". All nutritious food keeps your brain healthy and terms like "support brain health" are meaningless.

The same nonsense can be found in the "pop" psychology business. The goofier the approach the bigger the placebo effect, it seems.

Anxiety

So, yes, some people respond positively to placebos (the more suggestible ones, by the way) and some people get better due to spontaneous remission. If these things help, then terrific, but surely we can do better than this? When it comes to the anxiety-related disorders we certainly can.

Proven Therapies

The third reason people recover from physical or mental disorders is because the treatment they receive **actually works**.

The penicillin does kill off the infection, the chemotherapy does knock back the cancer, the anti-psychotic medication does reduce the delusions, the CBT does eliminate the panic attacks. And by "actually works" I mean that the person gets significantly better than can be explained by the passage of time (spontaneous remission) and/or the placebo effect.

In other words, if the treatment leads to significantly better outcomes than is the case for patients left on a waiting list or given a placebo, only then may we say the treatment is evidence-based. And, in my view, **only then** may we legitimately charge for it.

Anxiety

Rules of Evidence

Imagine, for example, if your local health food store only sold supplements that were proven in large scale, double-blind studies, to lead to significantly better health outcomes than do placebos or spontaneous remission. That would be great and I am sure some supplements do meet this criterion. One suspects, however, that this industry would shrink significantly were it only to sell evidence-based products.

This is why "quacktitioners", as I call them, use verbal "tricks" to fool people into paying for all the rest of the "treatments" that they sell. Amongst these are testimonials. If Uncle Fred says his memory improved after he started taking powdered butterfly wings does this mean we should buy some? Did his memory just get better anyway (after he stopped drinking)? Is he a placebo responder and after the initial excitement was he back where he started? Was he paid to say this? What if he was a retired sports hero or a famous actor? Would that make you take him more seriously? How about if he was wearing a white coat and had "Dr." in front of his name? "Doctor of what?" would be my first question.

Really, all I am suggesting is for you to select the "rules of evidence" that are in your best interest. Such rules would include that the evidence in favor of a treatment has been published in a legitimate, peer-reviewed, scientific journal and replicated by other researchers. Academic journals require that anything they publish has been carefully vetted by other experts in the field prior to possible publication.

Yes, I am aware that very occasionally incorrect information does sneak through that process too. The Wakefield study which linked autism to vaccination, and was published in the British academic journal *The Lancet*, is one such example. Encouragingly, however, this article was subsequently discredited, withdrawn from the scientific literature and its author struck from the United Kingdom's medical registry. Numerous, properly conducted studies have now shown, definitively, that autism is **not** caused by vaccination.

One wishes that certain celebrities and even a US President, who speak against vaccination, would avail themselves of the large number of scientific studies showing vaccines are safe, effective

Anxiety

and save millions of children's lives globally. Evidence-based research self-corrects. Non-evidence-based claims do not.

Via government regulation, pharmaceuticals are required to demonstrate that they are both safe **and** effective. "Supplements", pop psychology "treatments" and such, however, are subject to no scientific requirement of efficacy or government regulation. This is both disappointing and dangerous.

Another issue is the term "clinically proven" – one more meaningless phrase that simply says someone somewhere got better after taking the stuff. Better because their problem resolved itself? Better because their belief in the product made them feel better? Or better because it worked?

My point here is that evidence-based psychological treatments are widely known amongst appropriately qualified professionals and it is these treatments you should fact check and seek.

How Valid Research is Conducted

How, then, are the scientific studies of treatment efficacy done? How does a researcher find out if a treatment actually works and is not just a delaying action until the problem goes away by itself? Well, it is pretty simple, actually.

For example, let's say we want to see if CBT works for Panic Disorder compared to anti-depressant medication, compared to being put on a wait list for treatment at a future date (no treatment).

First we need to identify a large group of people suffering from this condition. Then, we randomly divide these volunteers into three groups: one group receiving no therapy (we will give them free treatment once the study is over), one receiving an anti-depressant, and the final group receiving CBT psychotherapy.

At the end of, say two months, we stop treatment (be it pill or CBT) and have all three groups of our participants evaluated as to their current severity of Panic Disorder by a professional who does not know which group they were in. We then have them reevaluated three months after treatment is stopped (anti-depressant medication or CBT), and perhaps again a year after that.

What happens? Well, as shown in numerous studies, the outcome is as follows: at two months, immediately after treatment stops, the groups getting treatment (CBT or anti-depressants) are doing better than the group who received no treatment. However, at the three month and one year follow-up, the CBT group is doing significantly and dramatically better than the medication group and no treatment groups. Further interesting is that the medication and no treatment groups are usually tied three months and one year post treatment. When it comes to successfully treating the anxiety-related disorders, CBT consistently emerges as the winner, especially when it comes to long-lasting effectiveness.

Unfortunately, and despite the overwhelming evidence showing CBT's efficacy, placebo "practitioners" abound aided and abetted by false advertising, "weasel-word" meaningless terms (like "clinically proven" and "supports brain health") and the internet. Google sources are especially troublesome in this regard though, to its credit Google Scholar (www.scholar. google.com) is often a good source of evidence-based research, as are peer reviewed academic journals. These journals have external experts who (blind, because the authors' names are removed) review all papers prior to publication. We now have a wealth of studies that clearly show that CBT currently is the most effective treatment for anxiety-related disorders.

Psychotherapy is Based on Science and Delivered with Art

It is true that psychotherapy and medicine, generally, is an art, but it is an art that must be based on solid science.

Just as your family doctor applies scientific knowledge and techniques to your physical health, but in an artful fashion, so your psychologist does the same thing with your mental disorders, occasionally in concert with a psychiatrist or family physician. Solid science does exist in the psychotherapy field and the techniques based on it are demonstrably better that those approaches that do not meet the gold standard of actual scientific knowledge.

During my 25 years of private practice in which I saw police officers, injured workers, military personnel, Indigenous people (such as Native Americans), crime victims, injured workers, automobile accident victims and others, it was abundantly clear that evidence-based psychotherapy, and especially CBT, was far and away the quickest and most effective path for helping these people return to a fulfilling and happy life.

It also was clear, and this is the central point of this book, that especially for people suffering from an anxiety-related disorder effective treatment had **vastly** more to do with de-bugging their mind than drugging their brain.

Freud's "Theory" of Psychoanalysis

Okay, so we agree that it is the mind we must treat. And we agree that any mental debugging we pursue must be safe *and* effective. Numerous mental malware removal techniques (that is, attempts to treat the mind directly) have been explored over the years starting with Freud's remarkably creative but unfortunately ineffective approach called psychoanalysis.

Psychoanalysis was claimed to be especially useful for treating "neuroses", which is what Freud called anxiety beyond what a situation requires, and "hysteria" (note that a "hyster" is a uterus, and there are numerous fascinating books on the history of sexism in psychotherapy).

Yet ironically, for the anxiety-related disorders in particular, psychoanalysis has been a failure.

It is wonderful creative writing (if you like Harry Potter, you will love Freud) but absolutely ineffective – and expensive, to boot – when it comes to treating the anxiety-related disorders. A theory is the best explanation of all available data. Freudian "theory" no longer meets that standard.

Freudian therapy was very popular with psychiatrists, though not psychologists, for many decades. However, most have now accepted that it is not an effective treatment approach. Further to this point it is interesting to note the word *psyche*, as in *psych*ology, refers to the mind not the brain, and further to note that *psyche* is also the root word in *psych*iatry despite that profession's current heavy focus on medicating the brain rather than de-bugging the mind.

For your interest I will add that some definitions of psyche also include the ideas of "spirit" and "soul". I shall leave discussion of those added dimensions of psyche to you and your religious beliefs and leaders. I am however interested to note that unlike one's mind, "soul" and "spirit" are conceived of as not requiring a brain platform to run on.

Other "artistic" or philosophical – as opposed to scientifically validated – approaches to psychotherapy also emerged during and subsequent to the Freudian era. For example, Rogerian therapy, Jungian therapy, Gestalt therapy, and so on. But none of

Anxiety

these has ever demonstrated scientific efficacy for treating the anxiety-related disorders. As noted earlier, of late some medical schools and psychiatrists have been taking a look at the convincing evidence behind CBT and are now being trained in its application, by psychologists.

My criticisms of Freud aside, he deserves tremendous credit for his attempt to treat the mind directly without the use of drugs. It was a bold venture but, ultimately, based on modern scientific standards, not successful. Its failure seems to have sent most psychiatrists fleeing back to their medical/biological roots.

Meanwhile psychological research has continued to run well and far with the "treat the mind directly" ball. Other approaches followed but it was not until the Behavioral (Watson and Skinner) and Cognitive (Piaget, Beck and others) revolutions in psychology that the first demonstrably effective treatments emerged for the anxiety-related disorders.

Watch out for Fan Clubs

Various other psychotherapies have emerged over the years with fan clubs surrounding many of them.

Good science, however, is not about fan clubs. Freud loved Freudians, Rogers loved Rogerians, Jung loved Jungians and so on. But nobody overcame an anxiety-related disorder from such treatment. My own, favourite quote on what research should be about is by developmental psychology researcher, Jean Piaget who said, "To the extent there are Piagetians, to that extent I have failed."

In other words, by all means, he said, look at my findings but then keep going, do more research, see where I am right, correct where I am wrong.

Good for him. That is how research and science in general goes forward. Data is gathered following a set of scientific rules, and over time a "theory" (best explanation of all available data) is developed to explain it. Further research leads to improvements in the theory and after a period of time sound treatments often result. Unbeknownst to most of the public, research on how most effectively to treat anxiety-related disorders has been doing just that for at least three decades and is getting better every year, as well.

Good research moves us forward. Fan clubs around the latest pop psychology fad do not.

The Ethics of using the title, "Dr."

Let me add one additional point to the above discussion. It is my belief that when you have "Dr." in front of your name it means that your opinions are not simply personal but rather the result of knowing, and basing those opinions on, a body of evidence-based knowledge.

That is, you have studied the research in your field and, in the case of PhDs, also have added to that knowledge base as a requirement of being awarded your degree. Family physicians and psychiatrists are not required to have done any research but do have to master a wide body of knowledge as well as demonstrate they can apply it to patients. It is therefore incumbent upon you as the professional to speak from that knowledge base and **not** to use your title to try to add credibility to *other* opinions you may hold outside your area of expertise (especially when those opinions are to your financial advantage or are your political or religious views).

My own PhD does not make my political views, religious views or even scientific views outside my field any better than anybody else's. This is why many professions, including my own, correctly forbid me from using my professional title of "Dr." should I run for political office.

Similarly it is unethical for me to push any "pet theories" I may have within my own field. If I have a hypothesis about some aspect of psychology I am most welcome to research it, present my findings to my peers and see those findings published if my peers find my methods, findings and conclusions to be evidence-based.

I should not, however, put untested hypotheses out to the public as though they are a mainstream, scientifically valid, part of my field. "Maverick" views can be a good source of research hypotheses but a professional is supposed to be able to back up what they say by referring to a body of science.

The Two-Way Street of Mind and Brain

It is important to add further that, for a sub-set of mental disorders, drugging the brain may improve the mind's ability to operate on the brain platform.

Equally true, however, is the fact that the mind also can change the physical make-up and chemical processes of the brain. For example taking testosterone, a male hormone but produced in smaller quantities by women as well, may increase men's and women's sexual arousal (though there is a big placebo effect here). But equally true is that thinking erotic thoughts will increase your testosterone.

This is a key point: thoughts can affect brain chemistry and even brain structure, for better or for worse, just as changing brain chemistry can affect thoughts.

Let me give you a second example of this bidirectional relationship between mind and brain. It is very likely that making a big mental effort to stop yourself from being an Eeyore ("It may be sunny today, Pooh, but I bet tomorrrrrooooowwwwww it will

Anxiety

raiiiinnnnnnnnn") may well cause your serotonin, norepinephrine and/or dopamine to rise.

What is interesting here is to think about which is "cause" and which is "effect". It is critical to know that there is a two way street between the mind and brain.

As psychology textbook authors Myers and DeWall note, "Brains sculpt minds and minds sculpt brains."

You can't, for example, tell your thyroid to make more thyroid hormone but your mind **can** cause your brain to produce more healthy levels of neurotransmitters.

This will not only help in the de-bugging of your mental malware but also change your brain chemistry and structure. This will then, in turn, help your mind run more effectively and less stressfully. We already know, by way of further example, that mice raised in a stimulating environment will have more dendrites (receiving fibres) on their brain cells (neurons) than mice raised in an unstimulating environment. This will allow for more connections amongst those neurons.

Both your environment and your choice of thoughts can and will shape the physical make-up and functioning of your brain.

The Power of Graduated Exposure

So, what does the scientific evidence say is the core debugging, or mind-altering, power of CBT?

As I noted in Chapter 4, it is:

> (a) the learning (desensitization) that comes through exposure, plus,

> (b) the challenging of catastrophic thoughts for their inaccuracy.

In my clinical experience some people get the most help via exposure and some via challenging their inaccurate and self-defeating thoughts, but for most people a combination works best. While exposure may seem cruel (rather like poking a stick into a wound), it works and is a key tool in conquering any anxiety disorder.

Incidentally, I believe this is why Eye Movement Desensitization and Reprocessing (EMDR), which some of you may be familiar with, sometimes helps. Its approach is to have clients speak about a traumatic event (imaginal exposure) while moving their eyes back and forth or perhaps engaging in repetitive tapping.

Just as penicillin works for certain infections, even if one wiggles one's eyes back and forth while swallowing the pill ("it's the penicillin, stupid"), so exposure still works if one does such eye wiggling. Or, for that matter, if one wears a hat with moons and stars on it while doing exposure. Several studies show that the eye wiggling (or tapping or whatever) part of this treatment is irrelevant. The active ingredient is the exposure. So skip the eye movements (though perhaps they add a placebo effect and/or give tentative therapists the courage to do exposure more firmly?) and get on with the exposure. "It's the exposure, stupid."

In conclusion, my purpose in this chapter has been to encourage you to take a critical thinking approach when you research what treatments will work best for your anxiety-related disorder. Such an approach will save you time and money and will vastly increase your chances of recovery. I believe that such investigation will lead you to place your bet on Cognitive Behavioral Therapy, but as an independent critical thinker, the choice, of course, is yours.

Anxiety

CHAPTER 6

FOOLS RUSH IN – SO BE A FOOL AND DO IT ANYWAY!

In this final chapter of Part I of this book I want to re-stress that I am not just addressing those of you officially diagnosed with an Anxiety-related disorder but all of you who find these and other types of anxiety to be a barrier to your full enjoyment of life. Please allow me to elaborate.

The diagnostic system used in the field of mental disorders was developed by both psychiatrists and psychologists, however, the *former* professionals played the greater role.

As a result, and likely because of their medical background, the relevant diagnostic system (DSM 5) uses a *category* approach rather than a *dimensional* one. Let me quickly explain the drawbacks of the categorical system and explain why I think a dimensional model is better.

With regard to diseases, physicians are used to a system in which someone either has a disease or does not. If the patient meets the diagnostic criteria for chicken pox (or a cancer, or diabetes, or Parkinson's) then they have it. If they do not then they don't. MDs apply this model to most all bodily diseases and malfunctions. Hence, and not surprisingly, they used this same "you have it or you don't" model when formulating a system to diagnose mental disorders.

In North America, this system is called DSM 5. For your interest, by the way, most other countries title their diagnostic system the International Statistical Classification of Diseases and Related Health Problems (ICD 10) and it includes both mental and physical disorders. China uses a third system.

Thus, in order for it to be "official" that you have an anxiety-related disorder, you must "meet the criteria" for that disorder in order to qualify for a diagnosis.

Anxiety

This matters, firstly, because many professionals' ability to get paid for treating you hinges on confirming that you do indeed have a mental disorder.

Additionally, and importantly, funding for treatment, or compensation, should someone be at fault for causing you to develop such a mental disorder (for example PTSD), hinges on having an official diagnosis. Furthermore, if you are charged with a crime, being diagnosed with a mental disorder might lead you to be found unfit to stand trial until such time as you are deemed competent to participate in your legal defence.

It may also be a mitigating factor in any sentence you receive. In Canada this would be called Not Criminally Responsible by Reason of a Mental Disorder, or NCRMD.

Therefore diagnosis matters. It allows professionals to communicate with each other and makes "real" what they are communicating about.

"Sub-clinical" is Still Upsetting

However, while all of the above is certainly important, in the real world (your world) and setting aside the funding and legal issues, many people suffer from milder versions of the anxiety-related disorders but do not officially qualify for a diagnosis. Clearly, however, they (and you?) still need and want help.

Thus, for the purposes of this book I want to stress that the same treatment principles I have discussed so far apply equally well whether you don't quite "meet the criteria" for an anxiety-related disorder, or if you do.

Whether your diagnosis is "clinical" or "subclinical" is not an issue in terms of you wanting to improve the quality of your life.

Reducing Your Anxiety Score

This is why many psychologists believe a dimensional system, rather than a category system like DSM 5 or ICD 10, would be more helpful.

Lots of people have obsessive-compulsive anxiety, for example, but may not meet the criteria for officially having OCD. Many people may be shy but this shyness may not be at a level that qualifies them for full blown Social Anxiety Disorder. Many people may remain upset after a trauma but do not officially have PTSD, and so on for each of the nine anxiety-related disorders discussed in this book.

A good case can be made that it might be more useful to consider a system where one is assigned a score out of say, "ten" on a particular disorder. If you get a "nine" or a "ten" on one of the nine anxiety-related disorders then likely you meet the criteria for officially having it. This means you may qualify for insurance-covered treatment, may be entitled to compensation if someone else's negligence caused the disorder (for example, via Workers'

Compensation or a private lawsuit) and such a diagnosis also may be relevant to lawsuits brought against you.

Anxiety

Panic Disorder as an Example

While my "out of ten" model is a simplification this is in essence how a diagnosis is arrived at. In the case of PTSD, for example, the DSM 5 diagnostic criteria include five main diagnostic features:

1) "Exposure to actual or threatened death, serious injury or sexual violence in one (or more) of the following ways" and then lists four specific ways

2) "Presence of one (or more) of the following intrusion symptoms associated with the traumatic event(s) beginning after the traumatic event(s) occurred" and lists five of these

3) "Persistent avoidance of stimuli associated with the traumatic event(s), beginning after the traumatic event(s) occurred as evidenced by one or both of the following" and lists two examples of avoidance

4) "Negative alterations in cognitions and mood associated with the traumatic event(s), beginning or worsening after the traumatic event(s) occurred, as evidenced by two (or more) of the following" and lists seven possibilities

5) "Marked alterations in arousal or activity associated with the traumatic event(s), beginning or worsening after the traumatic event(s) occurred, as evidenced by two or more of the following" and lists six examples.

DSM 5 also notes that the disturbance must persist longer than a month and "cause clinically significant distress or impairment in social, occupational, or other important areas of functioning."

Finally, DSM 5 says, "The disturbance is not attributable to the physiological effects of a substance (e.g., medication or alcohol) or another medical condition."

As you can see, PTSD has a very precise definition, but what if you have some of these features but not the necessary number for a DSM 5 diagnosis? Well, my assumption is that you still wish relief from your distress.

Perhaps another way of looking at this is that whether chicken pox (a disease) symptoms are mild or severe you still have chicken pox. However, for PTSD and the other anxiety-related disorders, "milder cases" permit no diagnosis.

This is why I think the category model has problems when it comes to the anxiety-related and many other disorders.

Anxiety

Better, as I argue above, to remember that people who don't quite meet the criteria for an official diagnosis still need help. And getting back to the central focus of this chapter, being a "0/10"on an anxiety-related disorder may not be the ideal state.

I am glad my dentist is moderately OCD. That is, that she is careful and thorough, but, since I don't want to hold my mouth open all day, I also don't want her to be a "10/10" on that scale. Similarly, a bit of a worrying nature about the well-being of your children or job or life is a good thing but being **constantly** wracked with anxiety and self-doubt about such things, and thus having Generalized Anxiety Disorder, is not. Being impaired by PTSD clearly is undesirable but remembering and taking lessons from a traumatic event can strengthen you. It can increase your resiliency.

Given the above, and this is key, if you want to reduce your "8/10", "9/10" and "10/10" anxiety levels, the fastest way to do this, ironically, is to put yourself deliberately into "7/10" or higher situations in the structured fashion I outlined in Chapter 4. With that, you will want to employ the cognitive ("C") techniques of CBT as well. The latter, in particular, involve checking one's cognitions and seeing if they are actually true and when they are not replacing them with ones that are. Self-talk like, "how many times have I had that worry?" followed by, "and has it ever come true?" are key here.

Now read closely.

You saw in Chapter 3 that anxiety is the edge of personal growth – and it is the 5/10 and higher where such growth occurs.

It is when you "step up to the plate" and are willing to put yourself into a situation that puts you into the discomfort range that personal growth occurs.

"But," you say, "I don't like feeling anxiety at that level."

Believe me, I understand. *But* being brave enough to put yourself in that range is exactly (and unfortunately) what is required to get your 8/10, 9/10 and 10/10 responses to certain situations and thoughts to drop to acceptable levels.

Right now, before you have begun the step by step therapeutic process of visiting that crash site, tackling those panic attacks, pushing back against the anxiety you experience if you don't do

Anxiety

your OCD rituals, avoiding things you irrationally fear, and so on, then you may indeed be in the 8/10 to 10/10 level of distress. I can assure you that if you will pluck up courage and follow the instructions I outlined in Chapter 4, then week by week these levels will drop and stay down too.

As I explained in the fear ladder section of Chapter 4, those of you currently suffering in the 8/10, 9/10 and 10/10 range on the types of anxiety discussed in this book will drop those numbers into a much lower range *if* you are willing to deliberately provoke some 7/10 thoughts and engage in some 7/10 behaviors. If you are willing to step outside your current comfort zone.

To say it again in different words, your freedom from an anxiety-related disorder lies in your being brave enough to go into the 7/10 range or higher and calmly wait out the anxiety that results, questioning the accuracy of your catastrophic thoughts as you do so.

Chapter 4 showed you exactly how to do this. Remember that if you can be the sort of person who makes a point of putting yourself into 5/10 to 7/10 situations as part of having a "go for it" life you will become much happier and less anxious person in *all* domains of your life.

Can't versus *Won't*

The above leads me to a discussion I was going to put into a separate chapter but when I tried the manuscript that way it seemed harsh and that is the last thing I want to be. So here goes.

One of the classic things one hears when treating clients with anxiety disorders is the phrase "I can't." As in, "I can't drive by where I had my car accident." "I can't stop checking the door locks again and again before bed." "I can't stop worrying endlessly about my children." "I can't go to the mall because I will have a panic attack there." "I can't stop buying things I don't need," and so on.

Let's think about this. You **can't** go to the mall? You **can't** drive past the accident site? You **can't** stop checking the door locks compulsively?

No. You *won't*.

See why I was concerned about being harsh? But it is true, yes? And that is okay because what you really mean is, the anxiety you currently experience trying to do (or trying not to do) those things is awful and you just aren't willing to be that brave.

I understand and I am not asking you to be. I am NOT asking you to suffer that much. All I am asking is that you work out the baby steps toward facing the full force of your particular version of excess anxiety and climb up that fear ladder one rung ("baby step") at time.

And remember two things: 1) no step has to put you past a 7/10 and, 2) that 7/10 will rapidly drop to a 3-4/10 **if you simply wait**.

If you can be that brave, master each step, and train yourself to have the supportive ("smarten up, me") cognitions I outlined in Chapter 4, then I promise that after a few weeks you will go, "Wow, I actually did pet a dog, did stop checking the door locks, did say 'hi' to the checkout person, did stop plucking my eyebrows, did stop having panic attacks, did get past my PTSD," and so on.

And please give yourself a huge pat on the back when that happens. In other words the solution to resolving anxiety-related distress in the 8/10 to 10/10 range is to be willing and brave enough to push yourself into the 6/10-7/10 range or higher in a series of carefully pre-planned baby steps.

Anxiety

Anxiety is Part of Life

And let me add another important point.

Anxiety is actually part of life and any attempt to drug it away will simply increase its hold over you.

Sometimes it is fun, almost always it is manageable, and occasionally it is overwhelming. Mastering the skills in Chapters 3 and 4 will guarantee you a much more fulfilling existence.

Please let go of the idea that a pill will do this for you. A little targeted brave behavior and brave thinking is all that is required.

Permit me to give you a more personal example. Some years back I was interviewed by PBS magazine and amongst the various questions I was asked was, "What is your career philosophy?"

"Fools rush in," I replied!

Now by this I don't mean I dive into water where I do not know the depth, but I do mean that I try to say "yes" to new opportunities that may come my way. Have I made a fool of myself – more than once! Have I found myself being counted down live in front of a TV camera thinking, "Why the heck did I agree to do this?" Yes. But also I have had some amazing experiences and succeeded at a fair number of them.

More specifically, looking at my own life and career as an example, I can remember many such "standing on the high board with knees trembling" events. The first class I taught, the first client I saw, the first time I taught on live, broadcast television, the first time I did a live debate in front of a large audience, the first eulogy I gave, the first time I accepted a large contract to produce and host an educational DVD and so on. Each and every time I *made* myself say, "Yes."

Now let me be honest and tell you that each of those "yeses" initially caused me a big surge in anxiety and I did suffer up front ("anticipatory anxiety", it is called). But after I had done the particular event... well, you already know. It (*almost* always) felt really good. And the next debate, the next television experience, the next DVD was easier. Sure there were embarrassing bloopers along the way but the overall score card has come out pretty well so far.

Anxiety

Let me end this chapter with a story about someone I know and who has given me permission to tell it; though, as with all examples in this book, I have changed several details.

This person and her husband were disabled and living on a very small income. They both suffered from a sub-clinical level of agoraphobia as a result of not being able to get out of their trailer very often and they both counted on their spouse as their sole support person and friend. Tragically the husband recently passed away leaving his wife deeply traumatized. Her agoraphobia worsened as a result of her loss and, combined with her understandably severe grief, she was experiencing overwhelming anxiety.

I had a long talk with her on the phone, referred her to the AnxietyCanada website section on agoraphobia and, together by phone, we worked out a "baby steps" approach to re-expanding her life.

I was delighted recently to hear from her that she had indeed taken a "do it anyway" approach to her fears and was pushing to expand her life every week. As an unexpected benefit, her taking on of her agoraphobia was also helping her move through the waves of grief she was, of course, experiencing.

To summarize, now that you have read Chapters 1-6 (and thank you for doing so by the way) you know several things:

1) Anxiety is *not* a brain disorder or a "mental illness". It is a *mind* problem that can be de-bugged quickly and effectively via Cognitive Behavioral Therapy.

2) No pill will make it go and stay away.

3) While currently, some situations may crank your anxiety into an intolerably high zone, you can fix this by constructing a "fear ladder", then approaching your particular form of anxiety via a series of baby steps.

4) "Can't" needs to be gently re-framed as "won't", then tackled one reasonably brave step at a time. Catastrophic thoughts and inaccurate exaggerations need to be challenged and defeated.

I often have students who say to me, "I *can't* write a paper." What would you say to them having read this book? Here is what I say: "I tell you what. Tomorrow by 4 o'clock bring me the title page of the paper with your name, the title of the paper and your student number on it and I will give you 2 percent just for doing that." Guess what: it turns out they "can" do a title page.

Anxiety

And when they hand that in what do I say next? "Tomorrow bring me the opening paragraph of your paper telling me the essay question you are to answer along the lines of, 'In this paper I will…' and I will give you 3 percent more."

You get the idea. Any task, no matter how daunting, can be broken into steps that do not provoke anxiety into the fight/flight/freeze zone (usually "freeze" when it comes to papers). Then each of these steps can be enacted with the rule that one does not think about the next step until the previous one is completed. Mastering an anxiety-related disorder involves precisely the same process.

In conclusion, it is a basic principle of life that either you are pushing the walls out and making your life bigger, or you are letting them close in and allowing your life to become smaller and smaller.

There is no steady state. Your job now is to master the principles and techniques I have outlined in Chapters 1-6 and to *go for it*.

I will conclude this chapter with one of my favorite quotes. It is by T. S. Eliot:

"How do you know how tall you are if you aren't in over your head?"

Since you only live once, why not find out!

PART II

CORE TREATMENT STRATEGIES FOR NINE ANXIETY-RELATED DISORDERS

CHAPTER 7

SUPPORTIVE RESOURCES

My goal in Part II of this book is to provide you with further details for to how to enact the core CBT techniques for freeing yourself from the debilitating effects of your particular type of anxiety or anxiety-related disorder. I will do this in three ways.

First, I will refer you to some excellent additional on-line, video and print resources.

Secondly, I will discuss what to look for in a psychologist if you are in a position to add such a professional to your treatment team.

Finally, I will expand on the description of CBT I gave you in Chapter 4 and show you how to apply it to your particular anxiety type. I will keep these chapters quite short and count on you to refer back to Chapters 3, 4 and 6 as well as look at the additional resources I will recommend.

If you would like further details about how to tackle the nine anxiety-related disorders discussed in this book, as well as advice on how to apply CBT to the particular anxiety challenge you face, let me re-stress that I think the best place to start is the www.anxietycanada.ca website. All material on this site, which was founded by two outstanding psychologists in the field, Dr.

Maureen Whittal and the late Dr. Peter MacLean, is carefully reviewed by an expert scientific panel prior to its inclusion.

Additionally, unlike so many websites in this field which are in part or fully sponsored by pharmaceutical companies, AnxietyCanada is not. It is therefore not beholden to any one perspective and instead takes and reports the outcome of research in this field in an unbiased manner. In particular I encourage you to go to the section on "Anxiety-Related Disorders" which you will find under the "Self-Help" heading. You will see a description of each disorder's features as well as techniques for mastering it.

In the case of seven of the disorders you will also find a short video interview with a top psychologist or psychiatrist about that particular type of anxiety. In addition, AnxietyCanada has an outstanding anxiety management app entitled *MindShift* that you can download onto your phone.

Also you will be pleased to know that there are several excellent Cognitive Behavioral Therapy workbooks that you can purchase. For a good publication that applies to tackling worry across all the anxiety-related disorders, I would recommend you to *The Worry*

Workbook: CBT Skills to Overcome Worry and Anxiety by Facing the Fear of Uncertainty, written by Dr. Melisa Robichaud and Dr. Kristen Buhr. This very practical and easy-to-read manual is an excellent tool for those suffering from excessive anxiety.

Another I would recommend is *Mastery of Your Anxiety and Panic*, by Dr. Michelle Craske and Dr. David Barlow. *The Anxiety and Phobia Workbook*, by Dr. Edmund Bourne, also is a very good resource.

Finally if "What If-ing" about the past and future is a big part of your anxiety then the *Generalized Anxiety Disorder Workbook* is an excellent tool to back off the grinding sense of worry and self-doubt that may plague you. Written by Dr. Melisa Robichaud and Dr. Michel Dugas, it is an excellent resource and many of the techniques in this workbook also are applicable to other types of anxiety.

I hope by the time you have finished this book that I will have provided you with sufficient information for you to tackle your particular anxiety-related disorder on your own. However, if you can afford a psychologist to help you work through the CBT process so much the better. Regardless, setting up and enacting the CBT steps as I outlined in Chapter 4 is highly effective especially when combined with the disorder-specific information I will provide below.

My advice if you do decide to include a psychologist as part of your treatment, is to look for two things:

1) Is the person someone you feel you can trust and relate to or do you find them too eccentric or unprofessional to join with in a therapeutic relationship?

2) Are they well versed in the scientific literature on the treatment of anxiety-related disorders, skilled at the application of CBT to your particular type of anxiety, and do they have a good track record?

Ample research shows that the quality of your relationship with, and the professional qualifications of, your psychologist are two very strong predictors of a positive treatment outcome. In my view your best bet would be a psychologist who is a graduate of an American or Canadian Psychological Association, accredited, clinical psychology program and who is, of course, a licensed member of their local state or provincial professional college. PhD level clinical psychologists are trained first as scientists. This means that in order to have earned a doctoral degree they have actually added to the body of scientific knowledge within the field.

Secondly, they have undergone extensive training in the application of psychological knowledge to real clients.

Thirdly, they have completed a significant clinical internship under the supervision of more senior psychologists. You might also check if they have post-doctoral CBT training on their resume.

You may also elect to include a psychiatrist in your treatment, more so if medication is required, though typically, for the anxiety-related disorders, it is not. To restate my previous advice, note that the titles "psychologist" and "psychiatrist" are legally protected in almost all jurisdictions which means it is illegal for anyone to use those titles unless qualified to do so. On the other hand titles such as "therapist", "counsellor", "holistic healer" and so on typically are not legally protected, which means that anyone (including people who have not even taken Psychology 101) may use them and say that they offer "Professional Counselling Services". This is not to say that there are not competent counsellors, therapists and so on but I would encourage you to

Anxiety

take an extra careful look at their credentials and professional associations. I would especially make sure that whomever you see is well trained in CBT. If you do the math, six to eight sessions at $150-$200/hr with a professional who actually helps you solve your problem seems a better investment than 30 or 50 or 100 sessions at $80/hr with someone who doesn't.

Something important that I want to add is that you can't help noticing that I strongly recommend a scientific, evidence-based approach to psychotherapy.

You will also recall that I indicated that psychotherapy is an art – an art based on science, but an art nonetheless. Further to this you may be interested to know that the more complex the anxiety-related disorder the more important is this "art" element of treatment. For Specific Phobia, Social Anxiety Disorder and Agoraphobia, for example, a fairly straightforward approach generally can be taken.

One (a) sets up a fear ladder and proceeds in a graduated exposure fashion to its top; and, (b) firmly and repeatedly challenges one's own catastrophic thoughts for their lack of supporting evidence.

On the other end of the spectrum, while reducing your PTSD symptoms also requires firm and systematic application of exposure via a fear ladder, as well as cognitive self-challenging, deeper existential issues also may need to be addressed depending on the extent to which a sufferer's entire world view may have been shattered. This may especially true, for example, in cases of military trauma or sexual assault. Nonetheless the core of treatment is the graduated exposure/cognition-challenging model I outlined in Chapter 4. Its application will certainly reduce your anxiety symptoms dramatically.

Regardless of which type of "clinical" or "sub-clinical" (see Chapter 6) anxiety-related disorder you suffer from, remember that the core thing that is maintaining and even strengthening your anxiety is *avoidance*. By not tackling anxiety-provoking thoughts and situations systematically and directly you are not going to get be able to back off that anxiety.

I am sure many of you have found some things that do help you to cope. Numerous options are available ranging from "just keeping a little Ativan in your pocket", to meditation, to various types of distraction and so on. Emotional support animals are currently quite popular. You are very welcome to keep these supports in place if you wish but it is critical to remember that if you actually want to "shrink the tumor" of your anxiety-related disorder then you will also have to do the *opposite* of avoidance, and that is graduated exposure. Things that help you cope should be **transitional supports only**. They need to be ones that you will back away from as you begin to conquer your particular anxiety challenge.

If you are tired of the mental and physical energy which your anxiety-related disorder is requiring of you, and the negative impact it is having on your family, friends and relationships, then my advice is to pluck up courage and enact some carefully pre-planned CBT. This may well make your current coping mechanisms unnecessary. In fact at a certain point in treatment you may wish to, dare I say *should*, leave them aside.

CHAPTER 8

SPECIFIC PHOBIA, AGORAPHOBIA AND SOCIAL ANXIETY DISORDER

As I noted in Chapter 4, Specific Phobia, Agoraphobia and Social Anxiety Disorder each involve an irrationally severe anxiety reaction to things or situations that are not actually dangerous. Examples I can think of from my own work include a mom who "couldn't" go camping with her husband and boys because of a severe but irrational fear of bugs; a man, home recovering from a severe work injury who gradually lost his confidence about going out in the community and ended up "unable" to leave his home; and a teenager who avoided any and all social contact to the severe detriment of her transition into adulthood.

So how do we help these people?

Anxiety

Step one, of course, will be for each of them to build a "fear ladder" with something currently "impossible" at the top rung and something above their comfort zone at the bottom. In between are an increasingly challenging set of thoughts and behaviors.

As you recall from Chapter 4, each of these "rungs" on the fear ladder needs to provoke an anxiety reaction in the individual to at least their 7/10 anxiety range.

The next step is then for them to deliberately do (or think about) the bottom rung situation and *wait* until their anxiety drops (which it will). Perhaps our bug-phobic mom could try, as her first step, lying on a blanket on the grass in her back yard or at a park. If that is too hard then she might begin by looking at a book on insects, picking a page with a fairly non-threatening bug (for example, a ladybug) and then look at that page and wait until her anxiety drops.

Additionally, as you recall from previous chapters, she has to take firm control of her (highly inaccurate) catastrophic thoughts and challenge them for their lack of truthfulness as she notes the non-disastrous consequences of her exposure steps. ("Gee, an ant was on my blanket and *nothing happened.*")

Comparing the **actual** results of the behavioral steps to the **anticipated** results is a key element in the CBT process as it proves to the person how badly their mind is currently misleading them. Perhaps our injured man could make his bottom rung to have a cup of coffee sitting on his front step or on his balcony. While doing this he can take note that despite his temporary fight or flight symptoms being unpleasant, **nothing** bad is actually happening and darned if those symptoms don't start to fade if he simply waits them out.

And maybe our teenager could make her first homework assignment to smile at a classmate at school the next day, note how that goes, and then try something a little socially bolder the next day and so on. Each step for these people needs to be repeated several times daily until it no longer leads to an anxiety reaction above a 2-3 out of 10. Once that step is mastered then the person moves up to the next rung on the ladder, follows the same procedure and so on.

Further to the cognitive part of treatment, it is important to engage in helpful thoughts such as, "This isn't so bad," "Hey, I did rung #2," and so on. Rewards for "moving up the rungs" are very helpful. Perhaps, for example, after mastering every five rungs you could purchase yourself a congratulatory gift.

It is also very important that family and friends understand what you are doing and are on-side with the process. Quite often they, unintentionally, strengthen your anxiety-related disorder by "protecting" you from things that provoke your anxiety response. They assist your avoidance. While their intentions are good, it is important now for you to tell them what you are doing and to ask them to support your exposure process rather than allowing or helping you to avoid your anxiety challenges. We all tend to protect those we love but "protecting" in this circumstance can easily become "enabling" which will actually deepen and harden your anxiety response. It is important therefore that family and friends know what you are trying to do and how they can help, rather than accidentally hinder the process.

Similarly "supportive psychotherapy" (Rogerian or humanistic, therapy) is the last thing you want if you are working with a therapist, as it supports the problem (avoidance) rather than emboldening you to tackle your irrational and imprisoning fears. "Insight-based" (psychodynamic) therapies are equally useless and counter-productive.

Of further help as you work up the rungs of your fear ladder is to use controlled breathing while enacting each step. As noted in Chapter 4, this involves breathing in through the nose and out through the mouth which prevents disturbing your oxygen/carbon dioxide balance. Positive thoughts such as "Hey, this isn't so bad," "I *can* do this," and "Be patient and this anxiety *will* drop," "Nothing bad is happening when I do these steps," and so on, also are very helpful.

One caveat to the above is in the case of the blood/injection type of Specific Phobia. These are people who faint when they see blood or needles. Interestingly, this response has a very strong genetic component. The same principles as outlined above do work but proceed with a little more caution as you make your way through the process of tackling a blood/injection phobia.

Clenching your fists, by the way, is a good technique to keep your blood pressure from falling too low. A full body clench, including the buttocks muscles, works even better as it stimulates your vagus nerve, guaranteeing that you won't faint, via raising your blood pressure.

CHAPTER 9

HOARDING, BODY-SPECIFIC REPETITIVE DISORDER AND OBSESSIVE-COMPULSIVE DISORDER

While treatment for many anxiety-related disorders involves building up courage to *do* feared behaviors, treatment of Hoarding Disorder, Body-Specific Repetitive Disorder and Obsessive-Compulsive Disorder involves mustering that same courage in order *not* to do a particular behavior, or *not* to engage in harmful thinking. This involves tackling not only the time-wasting and self-damaging *behaviors* of these types of anxiety but also the *cognitions* (thoughts) that accompany or precede them.

Anxiety

Thus, for the above three types of anxiety, the fear ladder you set up must involve gradually weaning yourself off the "need" to engage in these pointless and harmful behaviors and thoughts.

It is useful to think of these three types of anxiety as bullies. "They" try to make you do and things that hurt you or waste your time. Perhaps as a child some of you had a bully who made you take a much more time-consuming route home in order to avoid them? Or one who forced you to do something you didn't want to do. These three anxiety-related disorders operate the same way.

In earlier days of psychotherapy considerable time was often spent in exploring "why" such mental bullies might have come into one's life. The idea was that insight would then cause the problem to disappear. However this approach did not prove successful.

Further research has shown that actually it doesn't matter how you acquired an anxiety-related disorder. What matters is that you want it fixed. You want this mental malware de-bugged and out of your mind and life.

The process for doing this with the above three disorders is called exposure and response prevention. You *do* a step on the ladder (exposure) and *don't* enact your reassuring behavior or mental ritual (response prevention).

In the case of OCD, for example, where a person feels compelled to engage in unnecessary mental rituals and/or pointless physical acts such as constantly re-checking door locks or washing their hands far too many times a day, what they must do is to gradually boss back these mental and behavioral responses in the step-by-step process described above. As with all anxiety-related disorders this is done via "climbing up" a fear ladder (exposure) plus challenging untrue cognitions and taking strong note of their inaccuracy.

With OCD, one step might be to deliberately touch something "germy" and then instead of immediately washing, instead, to simply wait (while mentally challenging your catastrophic thoughts) until the anxiety response drops. And it will.

In the case of Hoarding, where people feel compelled to over-purchase and never throw things away, the process is the same.

Step by step targets ("rungs on a fear ladder") are set up along with a schedule to master them. "I have to" thoughts are examined for their lies and then banished.

Each step or rung on the fear ladder should provoke anxiety to at least your 7/10 range, which will then drop if you do nothing but wait. It is the exposure (doing the step) plus response prevention (no self-comforting behavior) that does the trick. If this process is set up and enacted properly the "bully" slowly but surely shrinks and loses its power over you.

Might that bully get stronger at certain, higher stress times your life? Yes, but knowing how to boss it back will allow you to promptly knock it down again.

The same process is needed in the case of Body-Focused Repetitive Disorder. Such people feel compelled (have mental malware that bullies them) to do damaging things to their body such as skin-picking, eyebrow plucking, hair twisting and so on. They report they "can't" (remember that word from Chapter 6?) stop doing them. And the solution?

Once again, 1) a relevant fear ladder is built, the rungs are climbed and tolerated until they become boring and, 2) self-defeating and untrue cognitions are challenged for their inaccuracy and replaced with truthful ones.

In summary, how do we help those of you who are being bullied by one of these three anxiety-related disorders?

I bet you now know. We do so by having you set up a series of increasingly difficult "rungs" which you will tackle one at a time from the bottom to the top. Yes, each step up the ladder will put your anxiety in the 7 out of 10 zone, but that is what we want. We want you to deliberately provoke at least a 7/10 anxiety reaction in yourself and then simply wait until it drops to a 2-3. You then repeat that step until even at the beginning it produces anxiety that does not go above a 2-3/10.

As you do a particular step you must *wait* using slow, in through the nose out through the mouth breathing until your anxiety drops. It will.

Also you must tackle your untrue cognitions about the disaster that supposedly will occur. It never does.

Each step on the fear ladder will involve one of two things:

1) Waiting a set period of time between having the urge to engage in the damaging behavior or mental ritual and doing it, or

2) Reducing the number of times the behavior or mental ritual is performed.

For specific help in setting up your own fear ladder please refer back to Chapter 4.

CHAPTER **10**

PANIC DISORDER

I once had a client describe his panic attacks as feeling like someone had suddenly pointed both barrels of a 12 gauge shotgun right into his eyes: instant, extreme terror.

Quite naturally people having such a severe response, which is typically accompanied by a racing heart, tingling sensations and chest pains (because they are unintentionally hyperventilating), often take themselves to a hospital Emergency Department thinking they are having a heart attack. And probably they should do this at least once, until medical evidence shows their heart is fine and it was indeed a panic attack.

A second version of this disorder is called Nocturnal Panic, in which people wake up in the middle of the night in a full blown panic attack that has no apparent cause.

Anxiety

A third variation can be people who awaken from REM sleep (where the body is paralysed) and this paralysis continues for a short while after they are awake. There is no danger here but some sufferers panic and then engage in catastrophic thinking which can bring on a panic attack.

Needless to say it is no fun being a Panic Disorder sufferer, but the good news is that it is one of the easiest to treat of all the anxiety-related disorders. And no medication is required.

Let me explain.

The unique feature of those prone to Panic Disorder is that they are much more acutely attuned to normal bodily sensations than most people. While the majority of people might not even notice if their heart skips a beat or races temporarily, those with Panic Disorder not only notice but then may begin the catastrophic cascade of thoughts and behaviors that lead to a full blown panic attack.

In the case of Nocturnal Panic, while most of us are unaware of our brains switching from deep sleep (Non-Rapid Eye Movement) to dream sleep (REM) or vice versa, those with nocturnal panic not only notice but, and here is the key, they instantly draw catastrophic conclusions ("I'm going to die") just as do people with daytime Panic Disorder. This thought then causes them to engage in behaviors (especially hyperventilating) that, metaphorically, pour buckets of gasoline on the anxiety (fight/flight/freeze) "fire". For our sleep paralysis person they too immediately start catastrophizing and hyperventilating, instead of ignoring the (interesting?) sensations which will then shortly pass.

So, if people with panic attacks are overly sensitive to normal body sensations and incorrectly interpret them as signs of imminent death then what can they do? The answer, you will not be surprised to hear, is to implement Cognitive Behavioral Therapy.

The "C" portion of this involves them *immediately* challenging their automatic overestimations of danger and their false, catastrophic conclusion that they are "about to die". Instead, they need to confront these inaccurate conclusions and to very firmly shut them down.

Anxiety

Self-talk (cognitions) like: "This is a panic attack, not a heart attack," "I am doing this to myself and if *I* stop, *it* will stop," and "This will go away if I simply stop catastrophizing and breathe calmly through my nose," firmly implemented will do the trick.

The "B" (behavioral) part of this, of course is the switch from gulping air (as the fight or flight response tells one to do) to instead breath calmly in through the nose and out of the mouth to re-establish normal CO_2/O_2 balance.

The other thing Panic sufferers need to do is start a program of CBT homework in which they deliberately generate some of their panic attack symptoms and then wait them out.

Among the sensations to which we want to desensitize panic sufferers are dizziness, changes in heart rate, feeling one is not getting enough air and chest tightness. All of these, I think you now realize, are a result of the unintentional hyperventilation and catastrophic thoughts that accompany the panic response. So what do we do? Well, the person needs to deliberately induce these symptoms and then control their breathing and *wait* until the panic sensations dissipate. And they will.

The actual process for enacting this desensitization process is very interesting. For chest tightness, dizziness and a racing heart, one thing CBT psychologists do, and you can do yourself, is to stand up and deliberately hyperventilate by taking in large breaths in and out through the mouth over an approximate one to two minute period. While you may be afraid that this will cause you to faint, actually hyperventilation raises blood pressure *not* drops it. So for one to two minutes gulp in air through your mouth and sure enough you will begin to experience all four panic symptoms: dizziness, a tight sensation in the chest, perhaps a tingling sensation and, ironically a feeling that they need to get even more air. But *this* time, instead of charging off to the hospital, you now know that it is the hyperventilation that is making you feel this way.

Next, you simply stand still, breathe in only through the nose/out through the mouth and *wait*. While doing this pay special attention to what is happening to your body as it step by step puts itself back into a normal balance and the panic sensations go away.

Anxiety

Since you know the symptoms were induced by the hyperventilation and, since you soon find out that your body puts itself back to normal after you stop hyperventilating, you learn two things. One is that it is the hyperventilation that is causing the body symptoms (in this situation and in your panic attacks), and the other is that stopping the catastrophic thoughts will then stop the hyperventilation and thus the body symptoms. The chest tightness and so on are *not* signs of an imminent heart attack but *caused by the person themselves.*

A second way to desensitize you to the dizziness sensations your panic attacks may produce is to have you stand up and spin in a circle (or sit on a chair that can be spun) until you become dizzy (dare we call this spin doctoring?!). Then you stop spinning, wait calmly and sure enough your body puts itself back to normal over the next few minutes. This process teaches you that it is *you* who is accidentally causing the dizziness which will quickly subside if you stop feeding it with hyperventilation and catastrophic thoughts.

Thirdly, you can get yourself used to the "not enough air" symptom by breathing though one of those crushed small straws one finds at coffee shops and seeing that a lack of oxygen does not need to trigger a full blown panic attack. Running up and down stairs and again waiting out the sensations that produces is also helpful.

These homework exposures to the physical sensations of panic need to be done regularly, which will increase your confidence in being able to master and ultimately eliminate your panic attacks.

In summary, the essence of treating panic disorder is twofold:

a) Discovering and taking note that your catastrophic thoughts are incorrect and replacing them with the correct conclusion that all will be fine if you simply wait out the anxiety symptoms, and,

b) Deliberately and frequently self-inducing the physical symptoms of panic by hyperventilating, making yourself dizzy, and/or breathing through a flattened straw which will prove to you that such sensations are no big deal and dissipate quickly if you don't continue to exaggerate, catastrophize and hyperventilate.

Do these things and guess what? Panic malware gone!

Anxiety

CHAPTER 11

GENERALIZED ANXIETY DISORDER (GAD)

GAD, characterized by constant worry and self-doubt, is very much a private disorder that happens in one's mind though others may come to notice that you are a "worry wort". Also, it may compel certain counter-productive behaviors. Like the other anxiety-related disorders, GAD is caused by bullying "mental malware". This malware tells the person that they "must" re-think and re-check all their decisions and actions. It plagues the person with "what ifs" such as "What if, my email gave offense," "What if, I should have painted the kitchen a different color," "What if, my mother has fallen," and so on and so on.

These "what-ifs" then lead to the person spending countless, pointless and anxious hours second guessing themselves and worrying about the future and the past to the detriment of their enjoyment of the present and their mental well-being.

Once again our now familiar friend, Cognitive Behavioral Therapy, can come to the rescue.

For GAD, the cognitive aspect of treatment is especially relevant because so much of GAD occurs in the mind. Bullying thoughts that "force" us to second guess all our decisions must be seen for the time-wasters and unhappiness makers that they are. They must be stopped: "Doctor, it hurts when I think that."

"So don't think that."

Much better are thoughts like, "Oh well. It's already done." "I don't feel like worrying about my kids right now." "How does my worrying help anybody?" and so on, are excellent replacements. The trick, then, is to step-by-step train oneself to challenge these "what ifs" for the life-spoilers and time-wasters that they are.

Additionally, one must learn to tolerate uncertainty as simply being a fact of life and not let it dominate our thoughts and compel us to engage in pointless actions. Uncertainty is not something to fix. It is part of life.

"What possible good does worrying do for us?" we need to ask ourselves. Are we really a bad parent if we don't worry about our kids all day? Worry about whether people at work like us? Worry that our professor gave us a funny look? And so on. Worry does *not* make you a better parent, employee or student. In fact it makes you a worse one – constantly seeking reassurance from those you worry about to the point (no unkindness intended) of being a pain in the neck.

Worrying is **not** helpful or productive and it ruins our life and those of people around us. Keep telling yourself this and get this mental malware out of your mind and life. Family can be a big help on the reassurance issue and you need to tell them that from now on they are only allowed to reassure you **once** and if you ask again they are to **refuse**.

GAD is a pretty crummy way to spend one's life and it is a major cause of insomnia to boot. Training yourself to stop worrying all the time takes mental discipline but like any positive habit you do it step by step and soon it becomes self-sustaining. Many people think that constantly worrying about family is a requirement of love. It isn't, and actually it is harmful to all parties.

Our second tool for tackling GAD is the "B" part of CBT, and that is to stop engaging in the re-checking and over-preparing behaviors that the GAD bully tries to demand. As always we do this by first constructing a "fear ladder" and then moving up the "rungs" one at a time.

By way of a specific example let's take the very bad habit of checking "Sent" personal and or work emails, texts and so on. Am I not right that they *are already sent*?! Sure you could send out another "corrective one" but this starts to make you look pretty silly especially if the "correction" has "2am" on it.

So how about instead that you begin by not checking sent emails after 8pm. And then back this off to 7pm, 6pm and so on until you no longer check "Sent" emails ever. I can promise you that this process will indeed play a huge role in debugging the GAD malware.

To further reduce your worry over "Sent" emails, allow me to give you a bit of advice. Regarding messaging in general, make it a

Anxiety

habit to keep any with emotional content as "drafts" and only send them 24 hours later if you still think they are wise. For my college students I make it a rule that I am happy to discuss their marked papers 24 hours *after* I have returned them. This way, my thinking goes, their amygdala has had its emotional reaction and calmed down. Hence their cerebral cortex and mine can have a polite discussion about their grade and my feedback.

For further assistance in mastering your GAD I refer you again to the AnxietyCanada website and to Dr. Melisa Robichaud's and Dr. Michel Dugas' excellent GAD workbook.

CHAPTER **12**

POST-TRAUMATIC STRESS DISORDER

Let me begin this chapter by saying that I am not going to oversimplify the treatment of such a complex disorder as PTSD. Nor can I do its treatment justice in this short chapter. What I am going to do is explain that the key components of successful treatment are graduated exposure plus cognitive self-reflection, and that implementing these *will* shrink the PTSD "tumor" significantly. Other biological, psychological and social interventions also may be required but very often are not.

Having worked as a Registered Psychologist seeing police officers, military personnel, injured workers, car accident victims, crime victims and so on, I would say that PTSD made up over sixty percent of my cases. PTSD can be especially complex to treat but the core strategies for helping people recover are all based on CBT.

Two cases that stand out in my mind were with workers who had accidentally killed a colleague. I am pleased to tell you that subsequent to treatment, primarily via CBT, each of these people successfully returned to work and their families remained intact.

You can review the diagnostic criteria for PTSD on the AnxietyCanada website or by searching for DSM 5 and looking under that disorder. You will note that it is reserved for those severe situations in which one either sees someone killed, when one is nearly killed oneself, or when one is a victim of sexual abuse.

In my experience the core factor in developing this disorder is when the person experiences something horrific that is far outside of their previous life experience. Military personnel, who often must live in exceptionally brutal environments, are especially vulnerable and, given the multiple traumas they have often faced, are particularly challenging to treat.

By way of example, think of a young adult from a nice family and community who goes to war and sees children being forced to carry explosives, watches people being killed every day, is injured by a roadside bomb, or sees a comrade killed. Or think of the person whose previous sense of safety is shattered when they are brutally robbed or assaulted. Or the child who is repeatedly molested by a trusted family friend or admired leader. Or the worker who is standing beside a colleague that is killed by machinery or a falling object.

Clearly, numerous issues arise in these situations above and beyond PTSD symptoms (self-blame, survivor guilt and so on) and must be processed. However, first and foremost, one must enact the core CBT techniques of graduated imaginal (in the mind) and then in vivo (in real life) exposure. This process you may well be able to undertake yourself but by all means include a good self-treatment manual and a psychologist if you are able. First and foremost, exposure *must* be done as it is avoidance that is allowing "the tumor" (mental malware) of PTSD to continue to impair a person's ability to get on with their life and relationships.

Such "tumors" cannot necessarily be eliminated but they *can* be substantially shrunk and filed away in a back cabinet in the mind so that they no longer dominate one's mental life and behavior. Sometimes, a few years down the road, they may knock on the door of consciousness again and one should expect and not shy away from this. Taking a little time to re-go through some of the original exposure steps almost always will "put out" such flare-ups.

A recent (highly modified) example of the latter was, let's say, a firefighter I had treated, successfully, for PTSD about 10 years ago. He had attended at a very bad fire that tragically included dead children being discovered at the scene. Recently this person came by to see me at my college office (I am retired from clinical practice but continue to teach university courses). He was concerned because his nightmares about the original incident had unexpectedly returned a couple of months ago. He had been to his family doctor who had prescribed Prazosin, an anti-hypertension medication also thought to help with nightmares. However the medication was not working and he wondered if I had any recommendations. My own view is that the nightmares were an effort by his mind (not his brain) to deal with what was a not unexpected re-flare up of his PTSD "mental malware".

I suggested that he might try backing off the medication under his physician's guidance and instead re-do some of the exposure steps he and I had done when I saw him originally. Ultimately this would include re-visiting the location of the fire. We agreed that he would drive toward the fire site and when his anxiety got to a 7/10 level pull over and wait there for his anxiety response to drop. He would proceed with this series of steps, perhaps over a few days (each provoking anxiety in the 7/10 range) until he could actually stand at the fire scene and have his anxiety not rise above a 3/10. Subsequently, he reported back to me that the re-exposure was tough but that his nightmares had now resolved. While at the fire location, and not unexpectedly, he reported that he cried, which of course also is helpful.

While people cannot always re-visit the locations where they acquired a trauma I do note with interest recent work with military combat veterans with PTSD indicating that "re-visiting" PTSD-inducing combat via virtual reality goggles also can replicate the therapeutic benefit of in vivo exposure.

Anxiety

Let me give you a second example of the key role of exposure in treating PTSD. In this case (again disguised) I saw, let's say, a bus driver who had been stabbed on the job. She was diagnosed with PTSD and referred to me for treatment. We began with the imaginal exposure portion of treatment in my office. After two sessions we moved to the in vivo (in real life) portion of treatment and via her employer were able arrange to visit the bus shed, privately, when she felt ready.

On our first drive toward her worksite I asked her to let me know once her anxiety got to a 7/10. She did so about a block from her work, at which point we pulled over to the side of the road, sat quietly and I had her do some relaxation breathing. Once her anxiety had dropped (remember, anxiety *always* drops, providing you don't hyperventilate), I asked if she would be willing to drive a little further. She felt she had done enough for that day (which was fine as she had indeed been very brave) and we agreed to repeat the exercise in a few days).

In our second in vivo session we got to the gate of the bus shed and once again, not unexpectedly, she began to have an anxiety response. Once again we sat in my car and waited silently (with her breathing in through her nose and out through her mouth to prevent hyperventilation) until her anxiety had dropped to a 3-4/10. I encouraged her to take strong note of how the anxiety response dropped if we just waited and she didn't hyperventilate.

In our third session she was able to go into the bus yard and we walked around the bus several times until, once again, her anxiety had dropped to a 3-4.

In our fourth session we both got in the bus and she was able to sit in the driver's seat. Again her anxiety went to a 7-8 but she agreed (this is very important) to stay in the seat until her anxiety dropped.

In subsequent sessions she started the bus and we drove around the yard.

At this point (and we had discussed this in advance) she agreed to have me play the role of her attacker and stand behind her. Once again her anxiety went up quite high but then dropped as she breathed and waited. We repeated this exposure several times and also she agreed to come and sit in and start the bus between our sessions.

Anxiety

In session 9, she got permission to take the bus out of the yard and we drove around the neighbourhood with me sitting behind her. Interestingly, and very importantly, she actually began to become bored while we did this. Boredom is of course the exact opposite of terror.

I am pleased to say that after 11 sessions, with her doing practice homework on her own between sessions, she, the employer and I were able to set up a graduated return to work. I accompanied her for the first hour of her first regular shift, which was set at two hours, and as I shook her hand as I got off she gave me a huge smile and a very rewarding "thank you".

I am pleased to tell you that this brave woman continues to this day to be a full time bus driver. She did wear a Kevlar vest for a few months and subsequently decided she no longer needed this support. She has now been back at work for three years and is very proud to be so.

This composite story is just one of many (auto accident victims, military cases, police who had attended at fatal accidents involving children, robbery victims and so on) where exposure therapy – taking behavioral steps and noting that disastrous consequences *don't* occur – was completely successful. Exposure done gradually, supportively, kindly and *firmly* works well. And in fact you can do much or all of it by yourself.

For our bus driver, like our firefighter, there were existential issues to deal with too. Before the crime she felt that as a compassionate person others would notice this and react positively to the warm smile she gave each entering passenger. In fact she had smiled at the man who subsequently stabbed her. Many times she had given homeless or distressed people a ride for free. Prior to the attack, her view of such people was understanding and not judgemental. She now needed to update her perceptions of risk and yet not lose the very caring essence of who she was.

EPILOGUE

GOOD LUCK

I want to thank you again for reading this book. I hope you have found it helpful and that you are now launched, or about to launch, on a successful journey to exile the anxiety *bullies* from your life. I also hope that a new willingness to "do it anyway" has replaced your previous caution and that you are now determined to live your life to the fullest.

Yes, it is tempting to "take a pill" for your anxiety and advertisements encouraging you to do this are seductive, but trust me, it is not worth the price.

It is also true that the route I am proposing is a harder one, *but only in the short term.* It has two huge advantages:

1) *You*, and not a pill, make it happen, and,

2) It works and *continues* to work for your whole life.

Mental pain is very much like physical pain. We don't want to mask it. We want to cure its cause. We want to solve and develop the skills necessary to deal with the underlying problem and not simply numb our symptoms. This is critically true as we all know the awful price physical and mental pain relievers continue to force us to pay.

I know, and perhaps you do too, far too many people who for 20+ years have been medicating themselves for anxiety and yet whose anxiety has only climbed each year, despite increases in dosage, and whose worlds have shrunk.

So why not instead give the CBT approach your very best shot.

With that said I will wish you farewell and good luck on the courageous journey you are about to undertake. It has been an honor for me to be able to speak with you.

Dr. Michael Catchpole

Works Cited

Adeniran, R. (2004). The United Kingdom and United States Health Care Systems: a Comparison. Home Health Care Management & Practice, 16(2), 109-116. doi: 10.1177/1084822303258617

American Psychiatric Association, & American Psychiatric Association. (2013). Diagnostic and statistical manual of mental disorders: DSM-5. Arlington, VA: American Psychiatric Association.

AnxietyCanada. (2019). Retrieved from https://www.anxietycanada.com/

Bartolomucci, A., Palanza, P., Sacerdote, P., Ceresini, G., Chirieleison, A., Panerai, A., &

Parmigiani, S. (2003). Individual housing induces altered immuno-endocrine responses to psychological stress in male mice. Psychoneuroendocrinology, 28(4), 540-558. doi: 10.1016/s0306-4530(02)00039-2

Bingham, W. E., & Griffiths, W. J. (1952). The effect of different environments during infancy on adult behavior in the rat. Journal of Comparative and Physiological Psychology, 45(4), 307-312. doi:10.1037/h0062513

Compton, S. N., Peris, T. S., Almirall, D., Birmaher, B., Sherrill, J., Kendall, P. C.,... Albano, A. M.

(2014). *Predictors and moderators of treatment response in childhood anxiety disorders: Results from the CAMS trial. Journal of Consulting and Clinical Psychology, 82(2), 212-224. doi:10.1037/a0035458*

Copleston, F. C. (1976). A history of philosophy: Vol. 4. London, London: Search Press.

Cuijpers, P. (2017). Four decades of outcome research on psychotherapies for adult depression: An overview of a series of meta-analyses. Canadian Psychology/ Psychologie Canadienne, 58(1), 7-19. doi:10.1037/ cap0000096

Cuijpers, P., Berking, M., Andersson, G., Quigley, L., Kleiboer, A., & Dobson, K. S. (2013). A Meta-Analysis of Cognitive-Behavioral Therapy for Adult De\pression, Alone and in Comparison with other Treatments. The Canadian Journal of Psychiatry, 58(7), 376-385. doi:10.1177/070674371305800702

Cuijpers, P., Sijbrandij, M., Koole, S., Huibers, M., Berking, M., & Andersson, G. (2014). Psychological treatment of generalized anxiety disorder: A meta-analysis. Clinical Psychology Review, 34(2), 130-140. doi: 10.1016/j.cpr.2014.01.002

Cusack, K., Jonas, D. E., Forneris, C. A., Wines, C., Sonis, J., Middleton, J. C., … Gaynes, B. N. (2016). Psychological treatments for adults with posttraumatic stress disorder: A systematic review and meta-analysis. Clinical Psychology Review, 43, 128-141. doi: 10.1016/j.cpr.2015.10.003

Egger, N., Konnopka, A., Beutel, M. E., Herpertz, S., Hiller, W., Hoyer, J.,… König, H. (2016). Long-term cost-effectiveness of cognitive behavioral therapy versus psychodynamic therapy in social anxiety disorder. Depression and Anxiety, 33(12), 1114-1122. doi:10.1002/da.22540

Anxiety

Eliot, T. S. (1969). *Complete Poems & Plays of T.S. Eliot (1st ed.)*. London: Faber & Faber.

Elkind, D. (1978, May 14). *The Children Man. The New York Times*.

Faria, M. (2013). Violence, mental illness, and the brain - A brief history of psychosurgery: Part 1 - From trephination to lobotomy. *Surgical Neurology International, 4(1)*, 49. doi:10.4103/2152-7806.110146

Hunsley, J., Elliott, K., & Therrien, Z. (2014). The efficacy and effectiveness of psychological treatments for mood, anxiety, and related disorders. *Canadian Psychology/Psychologie Canadienne, 55(3)*, 161-176. doi:10.1037/a0036933

Issakidis, C., Sanderson, K., Corry, J., Andrews, G., & Lapsley, H. (2004). Modelling the population cost-effectiveness of current and evidence-based optimal treatment for anxiety disorders. *Psychological Medicine, 34(1)*, 19-35. doi:10.1017/s003329170300881x

Jumreornvong, N. (2015). *Exorcism and Mental Illness Across Different Cultures [Blog post]*. Retrieved from http://web.stanford.edu/ group/hopes/cgi-bin/hopes_test/ exorcism-and-mental-illness-across-different-cultures/

Katzman, M. A., Bleau, P., Blier, P., Chokka, P., Kjernisted, K., & Van Ameringen, M. (2014). Canadian clinical practice guidelines for the management of anxiety, posttraumatic stress and obsessive-compulsive disorders. *BMC Psychiatry, 14(Suppl 1)*, S1. doi:10.1186/1471-244x-14-s1-s1

Koch, W. J., Douglas, K. S., Nicholls, T. L., & O'Neill, M. L. (2005). Psychological Injuries: Forensic Assessment, Treatment, and Law. New York: Oxford University Press.

Kodal, A., Fjermestad, K., Bjelland, I., Gjestad, R., Öst, L., Bjaastad, J. F.,... Wergeland, G. J. (2018). Long-term effectiveness of cognitive behavioral therapy for youth with anxiety disorders. Journal of Anxiety Disorders, 53, 58-67. doi:10.1016/j.janxdis.2017.11.003

Kökdağ, C., & Sütcü, S. T. (2016). Major Depresif Bozukluk Tedavisinde Bilişsel Davranışçı Grup

Terapisinin Uzun Dönemdeki Etkililiği: Sistematik Bir Gözden Geçirme. Psikiyatride Guncel Yaklasimlar - Current Approaches in Psychiatry, 8(Ek 1), 23. doi:10.18863/pgy.37237

Laynard, R., Clark, D., Knapp, M., & Mayraz, G. (2007). Cost-benefit analysis of psychological therapy. National Institute Economic Review, 202(1), 90-98. doi: 10.1177/0027950107086171

Lindsay, W. R., Gamsu, C. V., McLaughlin, E., Hood, E. M., & Espie, C. A. (1987). A controlled trial of treatments for generalized anxiety. British Journal of Clinical Psychology, 26(1), 3-15. doi:10.1111/j.2044-8260.1987.tb00718.x

McKeon, R. (1941). The Basic Works of Aristotle. New York, NY: Random House.

McLean, P. D., & Woody, S. R. (2001). Anxiety disorders in adults: An evidence-based approach to psychological treatment. New York: Oxford University Press.

Anxiety

Myers, D. G., & DeWall, C. N. (2015). Psychology. Worth Publishing.

Myhr, G., & Payne, K. (2006). Cost-Effectiveness of Cognitive-Behavioral Therapy for Mental Disorders: Implications for Public Health Care Funding Policy in Canada. The Canadian Journal of Psychiatry, 51(10), 662-670. doi: 10.1177/070674370605101006

Novella, S. (2016). A Psychiatrist Falls for Exorcism [Blog post]. Retrieved from https://theness.com/neurologicablog /index.php/a-psychiatrist-falls-for-exorcism/

Plato, & Cornford, F. M. (1964). Plato's Theory of Knowledge: The "Theaetetus" and the "Sophist" of Plato translated with a running commentary by F. Macdonald Cornford. London, London: Routledge & Kegan Paul Ltd.

Radford, B. (2013). Exorcism: Facts and Fiction About Demonic Possession [Blog post]. Retrieved from https://www. livescience.com/27727-exorcism-facts-and-fiction.html

Robichaud, M., & Dugas, M. J. (2015). The generalized anxiety disorder workbook: A comprehensive CBT guide for coping with uncertainty, worry, and fear. Harbinger Press.

Robichaud, M., and Buhr, K. (2018) The Worry Workbook: CBT skills to Overcome Anxiety by Facing the Fear of Uncertainty. Amazon.

Sagarwala, R., Malmstrom, T., & Nasrallah, H. A. (2018). Effects of nonpharmacological therapies on anxiety and cortisol: A meta-analysis. Annals Of Clinical Psychiatry (American Academy Of Clinical Psychiatrists (AACP)), 91-96.

Salzer, S., Winkelbach, C., Leweke, F., Leibing, E., & Leichsenring, F. (2011). Long-Term Effects of Short-Term Psychodynamic Psychotherapy and Cognitive-Behavioral Therapy in Generalized Anxiety Disorder: 12-Month Follow-up. The Canadian Journal of Psychiatry, 56(8), 503-508. doi: 10.1177/070674371105600809

Singh, N., & Reece, J. (2013). Psychotherapy, Pharmacotherapy, and Their Combination for Adolescents with Major Depressive Disorder: A Meta-Analysis. The Australian Educational and Developmental Psychologist, 31(01), 47-65. doi:10.1017/edp.2013.20

Siqueland, L., Rynn, M., & Diamond, G. S. (2005). Cognitive behavioral and attachment-based family therapy for anxious adolescents: Phase I and II studies. Journal of Anxiety Disorders, 19(4), 361-381. doi: 10.1016/j.janxdis.2004.04.006

Taylor, L. E., Swerdfeger, A. L., & Eslick, G. D. (2014). Vaccines are not associated with autism: An evidence-based meta-analysis of case-control and cohort studies. Vaccine, 32(29), 3623-3629. doi: 10.1016/j.vaccine.2014.04.085

Taylor, S. (2005). Advances in the treatment of posttraumatic stress disorder: Cognitive-behavioral perspectives. New York, NY: Springer.

Turner, C., O'Gorman, B., Nair, A., & O'Kearney, R. (2018). Moderators and predictors of response to cognitive behavior therapy for pediatric obsessive-compulsive disorder: A systematic review. Psychiatry Research, 261, 50-60. doi:10.1016/j.psychres.2017.12.034

Anxiety

Verret, L., Krezymon, A., Halley, H., Trouche, S., Zerwas, M., Lazouret, M.,…
Rampon, C. (2013). Transient enriched housing before amyloidosis onset sustains
cognitive improvement in Tg2576 mice. Neurobiology of Aging, 34(1), 211-225.
doi:10.1016/j.neurobiolaging.2012.05.013

Wittgenstein, L., & Anscombe, G. E. (1973). Philosophical investigations: The English
text of the third edition (3rd ed.). New York, NY: Macmillan.

Young, D., Lawlor, P. A., Leone, P., Dragunow, M., & During, M. J. (1999).
Environmental enrichment inhibits spontaneous apoptosis, prevents seizures and is
neuroprotective. Nature Medicine, 5(4), 448-453. doi:10.1038/7449

Lightning Source UK Ltd.
Milton Keynes UK
UKHW031054210519
343056UK00010B/2761/P